FATHERHOOD

FATHERHOOD

ED J. PINEGAR

Published by
Deseret Book Company
Salt Lake City, Utah
1977

*To my loving mother
and the memory of my late father,
and to my wonderful wife
and our fine children*

©1976 by Deseret Book Company
All rights reserved
Library of Congress Catalog Card No. 76-729
ISBN 0-87747-593-8
Printed in the United States of America

CONTENTS

ACKNOWLEDGMENTS

I am truly grateful to all the people with whom I've had the opportunity of associating throughout my life who have had an effect upon me, which in great measure is the source of the coming forth of this book.

I am specifically grateful—

To my parents, especially my mother, Mrs. James E. (Effie Jolley) Pinegar, for rearing me in love, teaching me correct principles, and encouraging service in the gospel of Jesus Christ. I am also indebted to her for many hours of research and help in preparing this work.

To my family, for accepting me as their patriarch, realizing also my many weaknesses and faults—

My loving wife, Patricia, whose love and counsel support me in all that I do;

Karie Lynn, whose internalizing of the principles of the gospel into her life have been a blessed example to her brothers and sisters;

Bruce, our new son and Karie's new patriarch, a devoted son of God;

Steven, whose attributes of perseverance and dedication and drive help him in serving the Lord;

Kelly, whose fun-loving and happy spirit adds the spark we need and whose complete and total honesty will bless her life forever;

Kristi, whose special deeds and notes of thoughtfulness come from a loving spirit that blesses all who know her;

Brett, whose love for the Book of Mormon and enthusiasm for learning new things stagger the imagination and challenge us all;

Cory, our gentle tiger with drive and spunk, who prays to be like Nephi;

Traci, whose gentle sweetness and affection touch all our lives;

And Tricia, whose happiness and excitement for life bring joy to our family.

I am also grateful—

To Elaine Cannon, without whose counsel and advice, writing and rewriting, this book might never have come to pass.

To Bill Nelson, for reading the manuscript and offering timely suggestions.

To Cliff Jolley, Stephen Oyler, Marie Payne, Laurie Harper, Margo Bodily, and Jeanette Jackson, for their help, counsel, and suggestions.

To William James Mortimer, Eleanor Knowles, and Michael Graves of Deseret Book Company, for their encouragement to me as an author and their professional contributions to the final publication of this book.

Chapter 1

FATHERS, ARISE!

Fathers, do you have any idea how important you are to your family? Ask anyone who had to grow up without a father.

I know.

It was 1947, when I was a young deacon, that the news came on Mother's Day that my daddy had died. I couldn't believe it. My very own father had passed away. I couldn't understand it either. Why should my mama and our family be without a daddy? Why should it happen on Mother's Day?

My angel mother raised our family with love—ultimate and Christ-like love. Her life was her children. Through her example I began to see the Savior's life with better perspective. He lived for us. We should live for others. And mother taught me of my priesthood duties, too. But superb as she was, I missed my father—and I miss him yet. Daddies are important to growing boys. A boy learns to be a man and how to father by watching his own, it seems to me. I am grateful for the memories of my dad that I do have.

I grew older and fell in love with a beautiful girl. Soon we were married in the temple, and the time to begin my most important role in life was upon me. I was locked into being a husband, a father, a patriarch in Zion. What did I know about any of this? I can't remember any of the advice I received, only a pat on the back and a rousing, "Good luck and success to you, Ed!" Thus I embarked on the most challenging adventure of my life in the gospel of Jesus Christ. I was now head of my own home and I hadn't even had an example to follow—just a casual "Good luck, Ed!"

In ten short months my role of father began in reality—Karie Lyn was born. I can't really say how many mistakes I've made, but probably the greatest was a lack of realization of what I was responsible for within that home. With that tiny baby in my arms I began to receive a revelation to my soul. I knew who I was and what I was ordained to do. The "magnificent obsession" of my stewardship unfolded before me, and my real life's work was about to begin. All the parts I was to play—son of God, husband, patriarch, priesthood bearer, leader, teacher, friend, and provider—came into my being. All my imperfections and inexperience and lack of true enlightenment on these responsibilities loomed up, too. But having a vision of what I was to do made a difference, even if it didn't make me a perfect father right away.

I recall visiting a ward Sunday School on Father's Day. Special effort had been made by the Sunday School presidency, the mothers, and the children of the ward to have all the fathers there to be honored on their special day. A young deacon was to give a tribute to his father. The microphone was lowered to accommodate him, and in a trembling voice he began:

My father is just like I want him to be. When he comes home from work we are all glad to see him. He kisses mama and lifts the baby up and makes her laugh. He runs his fingers through my little brother Jimmy's hair and says, "How's my little man tonight?" and he puts his arm around me, saying, "I am proud of my big boy."

When he is fixing things he lets us stand back and watch him. We like to do this 'cause what he does looks interesting and we can learn.

When he drives the car, he lets me ride with him.

If I have done something I shouldn't do he explains it is wrong, but he does it in a kind voice.

When he calls us for family home evening, we want to come because it makes us feel like he is running things in our home.

When we play "strong man" on the living room floor, he lets Jimmy hold him down. This makes Jimmy real happy.

2

When I fell out of the apple tree and broke my arm, he administered to me. Heavenly Father heard his prayer and answered it, for my arm is well and strong again.

The day I was to be ordained a deacon my father laid his hands on my head and gave me a father's blessing. His voice was so quiet, it seemed as if only Heavenly Father could really hear him. Tears came into my eyes because there was such a good spirit there, and I felt that I'd always try to be good so I could have the blessings my dad prayed for me.

The young deacon's voice faltered. He pushed back a tear and then, in a subdued voice, finished his tribute with "I love my father."

In the audience his father also wiped away a tear. We were all thoughtful. The message seemed clear to fathers as they caught the vision of their life's true work.

Later in the program the Sunday School president said, "Fathers, arise." It was time to honor each of us fathers with a special greeting card. All arose, but it seemed that after the young deacon's tribute it was with the question, "Am I a true father?"

My mind reasoned long after that Father's Day program. I have wondered many times since—I wonder now—will we men be worthy to stand on some future eternal day when our Heavenly Father says, "Father, arise!"

This is what this book is all about—how to prepare ourselves and our families for that day. It is a how-to book. How can we work our way through the various roles that are ours to play in The Church of Jesus Christ of Latter-day Saints and its teachings about life? How can we be successful as participants in the Lord's plan of salvation? How can we bring honor to our Heavenly Father as his sons? How can each of us become the best possible husband to a wonderful woman? What does it really mean to be father—patriarch in a family? Aren't there some special things a man needs to know to truly bless his family as a priesthood bearer? And what of our responsibility to lead, teach, and provide for our loved ones?

3

Surely the answers are all in the gospel, for this is God's will for all of his children.

It seems to me, my brothers, that the burden, as well as the joy, is ours. We must insure our own salvation, but we must also provide the saving stewardship for our loved ones so that we can all dwell together in the presence of our Heavenly Father.

I may have grown up without a dad, but I had a Heavenly Father as well as a remarkable mother, and I am committed to the idea that the gospel is true and the time is now for the priesthood bearers of the Church to take their rightful place as heads and examples of the families of Zion.

So, fathers, arise!

Chapter 2

FATHER AS A CHILD OF GOD

This is My Beloved Son. Hear Him!" Heavenly Father made this startling announcement to the world on several occasions. He said this when Peter, James, and John were on the Mount of Transfiguration with the Savior. (Matthew 17:5.) This most beautiful introduction was made to the people of the land Bountiful following the terrible destruction and preceding Christ's ministry among the Nephites. (3 Nephi 11:7.) And God the Father announced the Savior as his Son to Joseph Smith following the Prophet's fervent prayer in the grove. (Joseph Smith 2:19.)

The Lord Jesus himself has testified—the record is full—that he is, in fact, the Son of God. He has declared that "this is life eternal, that they might know thee the only true God, and Jesus Christ, whom thou hast sent." (John 17:3.)

One of the most important services of the Holy Ghost is to witness unto us that God lives and that Jesus Christ is his Son and our Savior. By that power we may all know this truth, and by the same power we may know that we too are children of God. Oh yes, Christ was the Only Begotten of the Father in the flesh, but Christ's spirit and our own were created, or fathered, by God the Eternal Father. Jesus is our Elder Brother. God is our Eternal Father. Christ has a special mission to perform, but we have our own missions or callings, and we can be strengthened in them if we have the testimony that we are children of God.

Everybody may be a child of God by birth, but we Latter-day Saints should be different. We should *act* upon our knowledge of who we are. I remember that I once put pennies in my shoe when I spoke to remind me of who I was and how I should act. It made a difference. The constant awareness of this fact can make a big difference. I remember the time our son Steve, then a young deacon, and I were riding in our neighborhood and he said, "Dad, guess who moved in this house?" "Who?" "President Brown's daughter—can you believe that? Right here in our ward in Provo, President Brown's daughter." I asked, "Who are you?" With some sarcasm he retorted, "Big deal, Ed Pinegar's boy." I smiled and gave him a more serious look and asked again, "Who are you really?" He was silent for a moment and then he said, "Oh yes, I'm Heavenly Father's son."

This understanding of our relationship with God is a special gift. Through the revelations given to us in the Church we come to know that this means we have the right to increase in capacity, in sureness, in effectiveness, in faith, in performance, even in quality of being, until we inherit what a son is entitled to inherit from his father—all that he has.

"So God created man in his own image, in the image of God created he him; male and female created he them." (Genesis 1:27.) A child of God! How wonderful! How marvelous!

Haven't you thrilled when your own little ones or a whole chorus of radiant youngsters have sung out with sweet conviction, "I am a child of God"? It is their favorite song. It is one of mine, too. They know that what they are singing is so because they are so recently from God's presence and they are yet unspoiled by the world.

Sometimes the best lessons strike home the most deeply when they are sung about over and over again. Consider the beautiful verses of Eliza R. Snow that we sing in our special gatherings:

> O my Father, thou that dwellest
> In the high and glorious place,
> When shall I regain thy presence,
> And again behold thy face?
> In thy holy habitation,
> Did my spirit once reside?

In my first primeval childhood,
Was I nurtured near thy side?

For a wise and glorious purpose,
Thou hast placed me here on earth
And withheld the recollection
Of my former friends and birth.
Yet ofttimes a secret something
Whispered, "You're a stranger here."
And I felt that I had wandered
From a more exalted sphere.

I had learned to call thee, Father,
Through thy Spirit from on high;
But until the key of knowledge
Was restored, I knew not why.
In the heavens are parents single?
No; the thought makes reason stare.
Truth is reason; truth eternal
Tells me I've a mother there.

When I leave this frail existence,
When I lay this mortal by,
Father, Mother, may I meet you
In your royal courts on high?
Then, at length, when I've completed
All you sent me forth to do,
With your mutual approbation,
Let me come and dwell with you.

Christ, our Elder Brother in terms of our spiritual creation, becomes as a father to us when we are "born again"—when we have come to a commitment that we will take his name upon us and will live according to his counsel, which is in accordance with Heavenly Father's will for us. And the more we strive to follow in his footsteps—to imitate his ways, to think, perform, and feel as he does—the more beautiful is our being. He is perfect. We are to become so. That is our obligation and our privilege.

And we are to help those little ones who came to earth later than we to do the same thing. Those spirit children of our Heavenly Father over whom we have special stewardship and responsibility because we are

7

their earthly fathers deserve our best attention and most inspired help. The partnership with God to help children participate successfully in life's adventure is the most vital experience a man can have. It is the most challenging and yet the most rewarding type of partnership. It has no rival in the business or secular world.

Let us remember the plan of life:

1. We are children of God.

2. Christ is our Elder Brother and will help us.

3. We serve as a kind of elder brother to our younger spiritual brothers whom we teach, lead, listen to, and perform priesthood ordinances for.

4. We have a special stewardship as father to those children who came through our own loins or who have been sealed to us as though they were ours from the beginning.

5. We have the goal of ultimately returning to the presence of God.

What difference does the knowledge of this plan of life make to us? What change can it bring about in our family life? What sort of comfort, motivation, support do we receive as we struggle along life's paths? What rights, privileges, and responsibilities are ours because we are sons of God? because we are earthly fathers to other sons and daughters of God?

This knowledge has incredible importance. God loves us. He counsels us. He covenants with us. He blesses us. He shows us the way through example, chastisement, and principles. He is preparing a place for us, for in our Father's house are many mansions. And he will receive us into his presence if only we will let him, if only we will try to be so much like him that we can be admitted to his presence.

You know, it would be a terrible fiasco if somebody were to go out on a football field, dressed in basketball clothes, and try to play soccer by baseball rules—or any combination of these games. Well, that's the way some people play the game of life. We must, instead, come to know God and that this life is his gift to us. It is his plan. He has given us the rules of the plan, or the game, and he has carefully explained winning procedures. If we have listened and will yet listen, we will become more and more expert and chalk up the score that marks us successful in this all-important effort.

We might continue the analogy to suggest that a father is a kind of coach. The more a coach knows about the plays and the more he studies and develops skills of communicating this knowledge to those for whom he is responsible, the better his players will be and the stronger his team.

Fathers ought to look to the source of wisdom, truth, strength, and sustenance so they can pass along the same blessings to those who look to them as the source of wisdom and strength. Being a child of God and a father as well means we have all kinds of special help, endowments, and directions from Heavenly Father.

Let us remember the commandment of our own Heavenly Father: "Be ye therefore perfect, even as your Father which is in heaven is perfect." (Matthew 5:48.)

Chapter 3

FATHER AS HUSBAND

A sensitive wife was paying tribute to the role of husband on a special Father's Day program. There was deep, responsive quiet as this sister spoke.

One of my most memorable beautiful experiences happened while I was in Utah Valley Hospital's intensive care section the first night after surgery for cancer. Momentarily I regained consciousness, opened my eyes, and there, leaning over the foot of my bed, was a heavenly face, radiant, anxious, beautiful!

"What time is it?" I inquired. (Always concerned about time—but why? I wasn't going anywhere.)

"Three A.M.," he replied.

Conscious enough to make a strong judgment, I answered, "Not many husbands would come at that hour in the morning." And then I was gone again. As long as I live, I need only to close my eyes to see that almost transparent, handsome face—showing concern, his interest, his love for me. How disappointing it must have been for him to see me close my eyes again after that brief communion! He sat in a chair in my room the remainder of the night, and several other nights—just to be near me.

Oh, husbands are important to wives! Consider this incident that happened to Emma Ray Riggs McKay, wife of President David O. McKay, which has become a classic in Mormon literature on marriage.

I accompanied my husband to a dedication of a meetinghouse in Los Angeles. We stopped on Wilshire Boulevard to get our car washed. I sat on a bench, and the President was standing over by the car. Suddenly at my elbow I heard a tiny voice say, "I guess that man over there loves you." Surprised, I turned and saw a beautiful boy about seven years of age with dark, curly hair and large brown eyes. "What did you say?" I said.

"I guess that man over there loves you."

"Why yes, he loves me; he is my husband. Why do you ask?"

"Oh, cuz, the way he smiles at you. Do you know, I'd give anything in this world if my Pop would smile at my Mom that way."

"Oh, I'm sorry that he doesn't," I said.

"I guess you're not going to get a divorce, then."

"Oh, no, we're not going to get a divorce. We've been married nearly fifty years now, and we are very happy. Why do you think that?"

"Oh, 'cause everybody gets a divorce around here. My Pop is going to get a divorce from my Mom. I love my Pop and my Mom, and I"—his voice broke and tears welled in his eyes, but he was too much of a little man to let them fall.

Then he came very close and whispered confidentially in my ear, "You'd better hurry out of Los Angeles, or you'll get a divorce, too." And he picked up his papers and shuffled down the sidewalk. ("The Art of Rearing Children Peacefully," in Harold Lundstrom, comp., Motherhood: A Partnership with God, *Bookcraft*, 1956, p. 63.)

Does your wife talk about you as Sister McKay did about her beloved sweetheart? Does your wife praise you in poetic appreciation? And how do you feel about her? Mark Twain once wrote about his wife, "Wherever she is, there is Eden." That is a beautiful tribute—and he didn't understand even the smallest portion of what the Lord meant a life to be when it was properly shared in the holy happiness of marriage! The promise of eternal togetherness, bound and exalted through faithful adherence to the Lord's principles and through his saving ordinances as we understand them in The Church of Jesus Christ of Latter-day Saints, becomes much more meaningful than a step back to Eden.

The ideal is to love each other enough to work at making a celestial marriage now, for joy today and with the fruits of it ours in eternal life. For such a marriage to come to pass largely depends upon the man to whom authority and presiding stewardship have been given by our Heavenly Father. The man is the head. He has final responsibility for the success of his marriage.

Remember, in the Garden of Eden the Lord said it was not good for man to be alone, so he created a woman and presented her to Adam as a helpmeet. When these two had taken that step which ended in their being cast out of the garden, God's significant counsel to each of them set the pattern that has persisted for the rest of us.

To the woman, he said: ". . . thy desire shall be to thy husband, and he shall rule [preside] over thee."

To the man, he said: "Because thou hast hearkened unto the voice of thy wife . . . cursed shall be the ground for thy sake; in sorrow shalt thou eat of it all the days of thy life. . . . By the sweat of thy face shalt thou eat bread. . . ." (Moses 4:22-25.)

In other words, the woman is to follow the man as he follows the Lord's counsel. The roles were clearly defined. Latter-day revelation and the teachings of the prophets have clarified and detailed them even further. Additionally, we have been given some powerful principles and saving ordinances in the fullness of the restored gospel of Jesus Christ, and if we diligently abide in them, we shall in fact find our own Eden today and ultimately our way back into the presence of our Heavenly Father, to rule and reign together over our own posterity.

How glorious a goal!

How perfect this promise!

How wise and kind our Heavenly Father is to prepare for us a plan that requires our deepest effort and complete commitment! This plan rewards us with consummate joy. In no other way can children be nurtured and taught by precept, example, and participation. In no other way can a male and female be honed into mature, beloved, and loving people fit for a celestial kingdom.

But if we are to have this eternal blessing, we must, of course, work for it, sacrifice for it. The ultimate blessing is to gain eternal life. It takes ultimate effort to achieve this goal.

I desire to emphasize this. I want the young men of Zion to realize that this institution of marriage is not a man-made institution. It is of God. It is honorable, and no man who is of marriageable age is living his religion who remains single. It is not simply devised for the convenience alone of man, to suit his own notions, and his own ideas; to marry and then divorce; to adopt and then to discard, just as he pleases. There are great consequences connected with it, consequences which reach beyond this present time into all eternity; for thereby souls are begotten into the world, and men and women obtain their being in the world. Marriage is the preserver of the human race. Without it, the purposes of God would be frustrated; virtue would be destroyed to give place to vice and corruption, and the earth would be void and empty. (Joseph F. Smith, Gospel Doctrine, p. 272.)

Our understanding and training, our thoughtful evaluation of the system reminds us that with the husband rest the keys to a successful marriage and family life. The Lord has so decreed. With his wife and helpmeet by his side and the Lord willingly and graciously there to guide him, he finds his task is sweeter and the burden of responsibility lighter.

If the role of the husband is so critically important, we brethren should be increasingly alert to home and family situations and status, to feelings and failures, to successes deserving praise that we have been too lax in giving before. We should be constantly aware of what it means to "husband," and what the scriptures say about marriage and family life.

And the Gods said: Let us make an help meet for the man, for it is not good that the man should be alone, therefore we will form an help meet for him.

And the Gods caused a deep sleep to fall upon Adam; and he slept, and they took one of his ribs, and closed up the flesh in the stead thereof;

And of the rib which the Gods had taken from the

man, formed they a woman, and brought her unto the man. (Abraham 5:14-16.)

And God blessed them, and God said unto them, Be fruitful, and multiply, and replenish the earth, and subdue it: and have dominion over the fish of the sea, and over the fowl of the air, and over every living thing that moveth upon the earth. (Genesis 1:28.)

Unto the woman, I, the Lord God, said; I will greatly multiply thy sorrow and thy conception. In sorrow thou shalt bring forth children, and thy desire shall be to thy husband, and he shall rule over thee. (Moses 4:22.)

And unto Adam he said, Because thou hast hearkened unto the voice of thy wife, . . . cursed is the ground for thy sake; in sorrow shalt thou eat of it all the days of thy life . . . in the sweat of thy face shalt thou eat bread. . . . (Genesis 3:17, 19.)

For the husband is the head of the wife, even as Christ is the head of the church: and he is the saviour of the body. (Ephesians 5:23.)

For this cause shall a man leave his father and mother, and shall be joined unto his wife, and they two shall be one flesh. (Ephesians 5:31.)

And unto the married I command, yet not I, but the Lord, Let not the wife depart from her husband. (1 Corinthians 7:10.)

Husbands, love your wives, even as Christ also loved the church, and gave himself for it. (Ephesians 5:25.)

Let the husband render unto the wife due benevolence: and likewise also the wife unto the husband. (1 Corinthians 7:3.)

Nevertheless let every one of you in particular so love his wife even as himself; and the wife see that she reverence her husband. (Ephesians 5:33.)

Women have claim on their husbands for their maintenance, until their husbands are taken; and if they are not found transgressors they shall have fellowship in the church. (D&C 83:2.)

And as pertaining to the new and everlasting covenant, it was instituted for the fulness of my glory; and he that receiveth a fulness thereof must and shall abide the law, or he shall be damned, saith the Lord God. (D&C 132:6.)

And again, verily I say unto you, that whoso forbiddeth to marry is not ordained of God, for marriage is ordained of God unto man.

Wherefore, it is lawful that he should have one wife, and they twain shall be one flesh, and all this that the earth might answer the end of its creation. (D&C 49:15-16.)

A home is not a home in the eye of the gospel, unless there dwell perfect confidence and love between the husband and the wife. Home is a place of order, love, union, rest, confidence, and absolute trust; where the breath of suspicion of infidelity can not enter; where the woman and the man each have implicit confidence in each other's honor and virtue. (Joseph F. Smith, Gospel Doctrine, p. 302.)

A Latter-day Saint who has no ambition to establish a home and give it permanency has not a full conception of a sacred duty the gospel imposes upon him. It may be necessary at times to change our abode; but a change should never be made for light or trivial reasons, nor to satisfy a restless spirit. Whenever homes are built the thought of permanency should always be present. (Joseph F. Smith, Gospel Doctrine, p. 301.)

The house of the Lord is a house of order and not a house of confusion; and that means that the man is not without the woman in the Lord, neither is the woman without the man in the Lord; and that no man can be saved and exalted in the kingdom of God without the woman, and no woman can reach perfection and exaltation in the kingdom of God alone. That is what it means . . . but it will be of no effect except it [marriage] be done and sanctioned by divine authority, in the name of the

Father and of the Son and of the Holy Ghost. (Joseph F. Smith, Gospel Doctrine, *p. 272.)*

Now, brethren, how do we measure up as husbands? How can we lift ourselves to a higher level? Here are four suggestions to help us meet these challenges.

1. *Count our blessings.*

Yes, count our blessings, and we'll find that our relationship with our wife is worth working on with all our heart, might, mind, and priesthood power!

Some of today's writers, research sociologists, and marriage counselors are taking another look at why people are divorcing in steadily increasing numbers, why some are avoiding marriage altogether, why some are living lives of "quiet desperation." They note that most couples admit to getting along great when they go off on a long trip or when they are together for protracted and protected periods of time. But problems arise when the daily grind drives them their own directions—and often in opposite ways. Fatigue, boredom, lack of communication, simply not knowing exactly what the other one is doing and when—all these can short-circuit the current of devotion and love.

The struggling Latter-day Saint husband and wife who think their complex lives leave them with too little in common should pause to consider a very vital fact: They are engaged in the Lord's work of rearing his spirit children in righteousness! This is far more important than any other work or activity they might do together or with anyone else. Couples in the Church who stay together because they "have to" also need to blessing count. A "have to" marriage is not a celestial marriage. A Latter-day Saint couple with a family have so much going for them that if they'll look at their marriage through the Lord's eyes, as a blessing indeed, they will all make their times of togetherness quality times even if the quantity time is limited. They'll find out how very much they do have in common.

So, brethren, let's start counting our blessings of eternal family life. And, while we're at it, how about the blessings of clean clothing, food, and someone who cares whether we get home safely or not in a snowstorm? And what about the very real gift and blessing to us of the woman who stepped into the realm of acute suffering and even near death to bring members of our own patriarchal line into being?

2. *Communicate.*

According to the dictionary, *communicate*—that very overworked and under-applied word!—means to share, to transfer, transmit, connect. This has to be the basis of a successful relationship of any kind.

Let me tell you about a way my wife got through to me (and it works the other way around as well).

Like most husbands, I suppose, I had a bad habit of forgetting to take out the garbage. My wife would frequently have to remind me. One week when I had forgotten again, she said, "You forgot the garbage again, dear." And the overworked, pressured feeling of an abused husband welled up inside of me at what I considered her criticism. I reacted to what she said. I didn't act! She could see how I felt and said quickly, "Well, we will get it out next week." The next week, the night the garbage was to be put out, my wife met me at the door and said, "Oh, darling" with great emotion! This caught me completely by surprise. She usually called me Ed, that being my name. Then, after the "oh, darling," she drew me close, gave me a long, loving kiss, and whispered in my ear, "Sweetheart, will you please take out the garbage for me tonight?"

I quickly broke away from the embrace, ran outside, took out the garbage, raced back as quickly as I could, and said, breathlessly, "Is there anything else you want me to do?"

The art of communicating with love and affection, empathy and thoughtfulness makes such a difference in how each of us behaves in our role of husband. What a blessing a sensitive, choice, caring woman is in helping a man become a more ideal mate!

Unquestionably, having prayer together can be the sweetest, most satisfying way to communicate. Every couple should begin at once to have daily prayer together (in addition to personal and family prayer). The act of praying together brings people together when both let the spirit move them to a more meaningful moment before God.

3. *Cherish her.*

Cherish is the word that implies the action that promises perfection in a relationship. It is another way of expressing love deeply and constantly. When a man cherishes his wife, he feels it is his privilege and duty to make her feel she is fulfilling her basic role in his life, that he is content with her. (Even if she isn't perfect yet, she'll get there this way!)

To cherish her means to appreciate the girl in her as well as the housewife, to appreciate her all-day (and night) labors, and her role as mother of our merry many. So we go on courting and complimenting, noticing, and showing forth increased gratitude with each of her achievements, from getting the ironing done to getting the kids all down—on time.

To cherish her also means to use our manly powers and presiding authority to help her. We should be the one who wisely gets the family members to carry their share of household chores. She isn't the head of the house, remember, and besides, most women hate to beg, plead, sulk, or storm. They may do it out of need, but they won't like it as much as our taking the lead. And they'll love us more for doing it, too.

Cherishing a beautiful daughter of our Heavenly Father, given to us as a wife, means that though we aren't perfect—yet—we are willing to humble ourself and/or arise as the situation might demand. Repeated efforts can insure pleasant habits.

And we value her sacred role of mother and saint, so cherishing her means that we'll protect her and safeguard her. We can use our priesthood powers to bless her when she is going to have surgery or a baby is on the way, when she is depressed, when she needs special spiritual strength. Some of the sweetest stories tell about a couple struggling in their marriage or a wife who is unhappy in their relationship and then she is given a blessing—a setting in which each partner is helped. We are her priesthood force that counsels with the Lord in her behalf, so we bless her when the Spirit moves us and how it moves us.

The presidents and prophets of the Church have always reminded us that love, like a tender flower, must be nourished so that a wonderful interdependence springs up between a man and a woman. Then it is true love, because it is based on faith, confidence, and understanding. It breeds unselfishness and sacrifice. When we so cherish our wife, and she us, we are moved through hardship, sorrow, disappointment, accomplishment, and accompanying pressures—and through time and all eternity.

4. *Counsel together.*

It is important to realize the great power and strength a wife can be to her husband as a patriarch in their family, realizing that everything should be implanted and brought to pass by the father, but revelation for the family does not always come directly through one single solitary unit.

To illustrate, one day when I came home, my wife said, "Honey, I feel strongly that we should sit down, counsel together, and set some goals." Now, we had always done this in setting the usual New Year's goals and family council goals, but never in the manner she suggested. We decided that on the last Thursday of the month prior to the last Monday, she and I would evaluate our lives in all the spiritual, physical, social, and mental aspects, and in every stewardship area we might be involved in. Actually, the idea of stewardship area was a joint idea.

At our first evaluation meeting, we decided on the areas we should evaluate—the spiritual, mental, physical, and social, and the stewardship roles of father, mother, brother, sister, family, in our work, our home, our church callings, and our other responsibilities. For our first goal-setting meeting, we fasted first. Then we set up our goals for our family, all of which were based on the relationship with Jesus Christ and being converted to his gospel, but which were simple, basic, concrete goals to which we could all relate immediately, things that we needed to do in the Pinegar family. We set as overall goals that year the development of honesty and integrity.

After this evaluation session as husband and wife, I then interviewed each of the children at family home evening the last Monday of the month. I helped each of them choose goals, and that is where I learned that goal setting is truly a patriarchal responsibility. Every child has a goal book to help him plan, act, and evaluate. Each child sets his own goals—some very simple, some very difficult, some long range, some short range.

Setting goals together as a marriage team can help us realize that we are truly one flesh as well as one in heart. Each of us can receive revelation, and then we can agree upon it together and act according to the revelation, realizing the great power of goal setting for husband and wife as well as for the whole family, collectively and individually.

"No power or influence can or ought to be maintained by virtue of the priesthood, only by persuasion, by long-suffering, by gentleness and meekness, and by love unfeigned." (D&C 121:41.)

Brethren, husbands, priesthood bearers, this is the Lord's best counsel to us. The 121st section of the Doctrine and Covenants holds all the answers, gives all the guidelines. Our task is to remember them and apply them in our relationships with our beloved family members. The Lord has blessed us men with the awesome responsibility of priesthood leadership, but he has also blessed us with a helpmeet who can be our eyes, our ears, our heart—if we'll let her—because of her innate sensitivity. She'll anticipate the needs of our children and be aware of our own needs almost before we are. She'll be conscious of special help suitable for our daily work, or how to magnify our church assignments. We need to counsel with her and then to listen. We are in this together forever. Making unilateral decisions is a sure way to make a woman feel anything but cherished.

Beginning with Adam and Eve and moving through all generations of time, on down to our generation, it has been the will of our Heavenly Father for man and woman to grow individually and to unite together in this most important arrangement of physical and spiritual sharing, of fathering and mothering, of parenting and teaching, of leading and defending, of supporting, and of loving, all within our own homes and ultimately with all mankind, as we come to know and love the Lord more completely.

The Lord has established the system and the safeguards. As we live the laws surrounding a holy marriage relationship, our testimony of the system increases.

It is man's joy to be married, but he must strive with his wife to apply the principles to the details, and he must use the leadership his stewardship demands to bring about success in this special calling. If we consider our wife as our true partner with God, and if we so live that the Holy Ghost tarries with us, we will be responsive to the promptings of the Spirit, and our lives will be the proof of this.

We must let no one or no thing come between us and our togetherness. That goes for children, worldly goods, and church assignments—even football, or golf, or fishing! We must allow for each other's uniqueness and help each other develop to the full measure of our creation. We must count our blessings for each other, communicate carefully and prayerfully, cherish and counsel together.

Brethren, if our marriage is sealed in the temple under the appropriate authority, if we keep the commandments, if we are involved in this most sacred experience of marriage, we will be able to lead our family back through the gates of heaven. If we don't succeed at this role, we've wasted the highest promise of our priesthood.

Chapter 4

FATHER AS PATRIARCH

What are you going to be when you grow up?" the kindly neighbor asked the little boy clomping down the block in his father's shoes, a tie looped about his neck with a man-sized belt buckled so tightly about his small waist the end dragged behind him.

"I'm going to be a daddy. See?" And then, very solemnly, the boy said to the man, "And what are you going to be when *you* grow up?"

The man was startled by such a precocious response. Yet it caused him to stretch his mind into eternity, and he admitted to himself that he indeed did have some growing to do. He replied seriously, "I am going to be a father."

An understanding of the eternal plan reminds us that one doesn't dream of becoming a heavenly school-teacher or a heavenly land developer, business executive, or dentist. Rather, we should be dreaming and striving to become a patriarch to our own posterity. An exalted life—a life forever in the presence of God, our Father in heaven, with us standing at the head of our own chain of descendants—requires that a man become a heavenly father. We become so by remembering and applying the supreme example of the Savior when he said, "What manner of men ought ye to be? Verily I say unto you, even as I am." (3 Nephi 27:27.)

There is no greater goal than to strive valiantly to become like unto our eternal parents. If we do not become so, we cannot dwell with them.

When we finally came to appreciate the importance of the family organization with the father or patriarch presiding, we will concomitantly appreciate the fact that there is no higher office or title in the priest-hood—or in life—than that of a righteous father. Of all the titles of honor and admiration that could be given him, God himself chose to be called simply Father.

President Brigham Young substantiated the pre-eminence of the office of father, with its eternal rami-fication:

We have not yet received our kingdoms, neither will we, until we have finished our work on the earth, passed through the ordeals, are brought up by the power of the resurrection, and are crowned with glory and eternal lives. Then he that has overcome and is found worthy, will be made a king of kings, and lord of lords over his own posterity, or in other words: A father of fathers. (Journal of Discourses, 10:355.)

Admiral Richard E. Byrd was alone at Ross Barrier in the midst of a terrible antarctic storm. The tempera-ture was 72 degrees below, the stove in his meager shelter was faulty, and carbon monoxide threatened his life, but he did survive and lived to write his book *Alone.*

While keeping his lonely vigil in that far part of our universe, he meditated and then wrote these words, deep with meaning, for to him his role of father and husband was the supreme value and joy in his life:

At the end only two things really matter to a man, regardless of who he is, and they are the affection and understanding of his family.

Anything and everything else he creates are insubstantial, they are ships given over to the mercy of the winds and tides of prejudice. But the family is an everlasting anchorage, a quiet harbor where a man's ship can be left to swing in the moorings of pride and loyalty.

There is no greater joy than witnessing the young son standing in Sunday School on Father's Day and say-ing, "My dad is the greatest dad that ever lived because he taught me the gospel of Jesus Christ." Or the missionary at his farewell, who brought his father to tears with this tribute: "My dad was my friend. We al-

23

ways did things together. I believe we'll still be doing things together in this my new activity." Or the beautiful young bride-to-be, bearing her testimony for the last time in her home ward, who tearfully turned toward her father and said, "My whole concept of Heavenly Father has come about in my life because of the kind of person my father is. That is the kind of man I looked for to marry. Though my fiance doesn't know what my father knows about 'fathering,' he seems to understand the patriarchal role already, and that is important to me, a woman."

The joy in being a proper patriarch comes home to the heart one blessed day.

Phil was a young man who had struggled desperately with the drug habit. He had spent time in corrective institutions, and his family's resources had been greatly whittled by therapeutic, medical, and psychiatric fees. Then one day, when he himself was at last in a position of doing clinical duty for a graduate counseling degree, he was asked by a teenage addict how he had made it through the horrors of withdrawal and the building of self-control.

"I'd never have made it if my father hadn't helped me," he said.

"Helped you? How? My father is part of my problem," the young man declared.

"He prayed like an old-fashioned patriarch. He prayed and he listened to the Lord. He prayed about 'our course of action' to help me kick the habit, as if we were in it together. He prayed over me, that I'd respond to treatment; he prayed for the professionals aiding me, and that I'd be able to resist temptation and hang on—that I'd try. He laid his hands upon my head and called upon the Lord to bless and heal me."

How superb a human being, how fine a father who promises his children that in no way is the adversary going to have claim on them! One father whose son was being threatened said to him, "Son, I'm giving you fair warning. I will never leave your side until you are back in the fold. I will personally pray, prepare, and tutor you. I will comfort and counsel you. Together we'll both grow closer to what God wants us to be. Now forgive me, my son, forgive me for past neglect that has helped to bring us both to this tragic but blessed awakening."

And the father kept his word. These two were subsequently seen everywhere together—on business trips, at the store, at the gymnasium, at the library, on the welfare project, in gatherings where the gospel was taught, and in traditional church meetings.

Fathering is forever.

In the Doctrine and Covenants we read: "And now a commandment I give unto you—if you will be delivered you shall set in order your own house, for there are many things that are not right in your house." (D&C 93:43.)

To the head of the house, the patriarch in fact or in priesthood line, rests this responsibility.

Who and what is a patriarch?

Traditionally, the role of a patriarch has been synonymous with ultimate political and religious leadership over a race, clan, or familial group, like Adam or Noah. The patriarchal order has always been the form of government for the children of God, as recorded in sacred scripture in the Bible and the Book of Mormon. This same system of government will abide in eternity.

The word *patriarchal* itself stems from the root *patria*, meaning lineage or family, and *archeis*, meaning to rule. In our own day a father is a patriarch, and within the framework of his own family, he claims ultimate leadership. In the church of Jesus Christ there is an additional definition. A patriarch is one especially called and ordained in the Melchizedek Priesthood to bless worthy members under inspiration from the Lord. Such blessings are recorded and on file in the church archives.

Prophets, leaders, and great teachers in the kingdom of the Lord on earth have always taught that the order of God's government, both in time and in eternity, is based upon the family unit. It is a patriarchal or fatherly government. Each worthy father who is raised from the dead and is heir to celestial glory in all its fullness will preside over his own children and over all the offspring of his children and his children's children forever and always.

This patriarchal order was taught to Adam and Eve in the Garden of Eden by the Lord and is the ideal form of government, but because of the wickedness and apostasy among succeeding generations, it had to be abandoned as a political system. However, it has always been maintained within the family circle itself among the Lord's children on earth.

The heart rings with tenderness when the little Primary children sing "I Am a Child of God." This statement is true. We were created by God and a Heavenly Mother in the spirit world before this earthly one. When this testimony burns within us and we take that understanding to the next logical step, we want to be reunited with Heavenly Father. We yearn for the blessings that Brigham Young so eloquently described in the following statement:

When we get home to our Father and God will we not wish to be in the family? Will it not be our highest ambition and desire to be reckoned as the sons of the living God, as the daughters of the Almighty, with a right to the household, and the faith that belongs to the household, heirs of the Father, His goods, His wealth, His power, His excellency, His knowledge and wisdom? Ought it not be our highest ambition to attain this?

If the only way to reap such rewards is to become a father like unto our Heavenly Father, then we should waste no time in the effort. Dreaming of being the world's best attorney, athlete, or businessman "when I grow up" pales by comparison to the eternal picture of basking forever in the association of those dear ones we've labored with, sacrificed for, prayed over, and, in fact, initially created in an act of love with a beloved wife and in partnership with God.

A true father/patriarch knows his rightful and blessed calling and stewardship, for he has studied and prayed to find out. He sees this opportunity as being one with eternal ramifications. He is preparing himself constantly to perform to the end that his posterity will gather together one day and dwell in the presence of Heavenly Father. Then, as the Savior said to the Nephites (see 3 Nephi 17:20), the father-patriarch can say to himself, "And now, behold, my joy is full."

Every trial and temptation, striving and struggle can be a growing, motivating experience in drawing us closer to the Lord as our spirit is refined. Every principle of the gospel is to help us and our family members realize this exalted and joyful state.

We can make out of our home and family what we will. Those who willfully choose to disregard this divine system, for whatever reason, are out of harmony with the purposes of God. All family members should try to understand the principle of patriarchal authority in the home. It isn't a matter of who is the most worthy or qualified or what church job one holds now; it is a matter of law and orderliness.

1. A father/patriarch should preside in his own home. No other authority is paramount in family and home affairs. It is our right to so preside, and we should not leave it to others. This situation is one that must be carefully cultivated to bring the desired blessings in peaceful relationships and wise decisions. The Lord wants order, not confusion or chaos, so family roles are clearly defined.

President Joseph F. Smith frequently emphasized the importance of a father's role:

This authority carries with it a responsibility and a grave one, as well as its rights and privileges, and men can not be too exemplary in their lives, nor fit themselves too carefully to live in harmony with this important and God-ordained rule of conduct in the family organization. (Gospel Doctrine, pp. 287-88.)

2. A father/patriarch should be more humble, more gracious in authority, more sensitive to the needs and problems of his family members. We must be converted to Christ-like principles and the application of them in our dealings with others, or the consequences will be severe.

3. A father/patriarch should strive to so perfect his

life that the Holy Ghost will tarry with him. In today's world a father/patriarch needs all the help he can get to keep the adversary under control and to provide an environment in which his family can spiritually flourish.

The father who keeps the commandments of God shall have the Holy Ghost as his constant companion. Then he must live in tune, constantly seeking direction through the Spirit so that he will be responsive to the promptings when they come.

The father/patriarch should study and pray so revelation from the Lord will come for the benefit of his family members. He can then anticipate their needs and be quickened to their problems unto their salvation.

One day my daughter Kristi came home from Primary in tears. This was a common occurrence; she usually cried during Primary and Junior Sunday School, for she was having a hard time getting used to going to her classes alone. Each child is different, and this was one of the differences in Kristi. That night she came home with tears in her eyes and said, "Daddy, I want to go to Primary and I want to go to Junior Sunday School, but I am afraid, and I cry too much. Could Heavenly Father help me so I won't cry and I won't be afraid?" I said, "Yes, I am sure Heavenly Father will bless you so you can do that. Let's pray in family prayer and in our individual prayers every day to help you be able to have a good time at Sunday School and Primary without crying." That night and each ensuing day we prayed for Kristi, individually and as a family. A week went by, and Junior Sunday School had passed and Primary had just finished. Kristi came running in the door. "Daddy, daddy, guess what!" "What, Kristi?" "Heavenly Father loves me." "Oh, Kristi, that is so wonderful! Tell me about it." Then she proceeded to tell me how she knew Heavenly Father loved her—because in Junior Sunday School and in Primary she hadn't cried once and she hadn't been afraid.

Yes, Heavenly Father can help us in all things we do and in all our problems.

4. A father/patriarch should respond to the promptings of the Spirit. He should have the courage to

act in faith, believing that the Lord lives and loves and "giveth no commandments unto the children of men, save he shall prepare a way for them that they may accomplish the thing which he commandeth them." (1 Nephi 3:7.)

While praying about a most urgent problem in our family once, I felt the quickening of the Spirit directing me to that which I should do. However, I lacked the courage to do it, and the ensuing problem resulted in a magnitude of sorrow. The hardship of learning (for which I am now grateful) and of experience did produce good results. I learned the hard way that when the Lord chastizes us for being disobedient, oftentimes it is in a most sorrowful situation. When we take the time to pray and ask for help and then the Lord inspires us with certain direction, we must have the courage to be obedient to this inspiration. If we don't, the greatest sorrow is in our disobedience to the Lord.

In the Lord's powerful plan, he has not required it of us to preside as father/patriarch alone, without help or counsel. He has given us the gift of the Holy Ghost. He has also blessed each of us with a wife, a companion, a partner, a sweetheart, a comforter and counselor. She should be the best friend we have, and we should accept her as a gift from God, with thankfulness and in deepest love. Together we should work out the affairs of our family in righteousness. We should seek her feelings, her wisdom, her innate sense on matters, and then determine, with the Lord's help, the course to follow.

Let us remember that a father/patriarch is accountable for the stewardship of his family given to him by God. There will surely come a day when each of us will make our own report before God. And what, brethren, will we say about our wife and our children?

God's system is the patriarchal system. He knows what is best for each of us. His principles are timeless, and they work. This is substantiated over and over again in personal witness, in the experiences of others, in the scriptures, and in the teachings of the prophets.

The blessed purpose of family life is to help each of us strive for perfection, moving confidently in the direction of becoming a celestial-type person. Unless we really don't care much for our wife and children, we will begin now to work with all we have and to live and act as a true father/patriarch.

Generally speaking, we know what a father/patriarch is to do, but what about our own family needs? Is our wife burdened with too many home duties and too little help? Is she disgruntled in carrying the load of house, home, children, and too many major family decisions? Does she feel less valuable to us than the football game on TV, our overtime work to buy a new boat, our over-zealousness with our church assignments?

Are we on good, close terms with our children? Have we figured out a way to consistently—and happily—get our family together for prayer and gospel discussion?

Honestly, now, taking a long-range view of things, an eternal perspective, don't we have the greatest family anywhere? We would do anything to insure a foreverness relationship with them, wouldn't we—even to working harder to grow in our role as father/patriarch?

The Lord has shown the way, and he will bless each effort we make in the right direction. Then, line upon line, precept upon precept, we can increase in understanding, commitment, and completeness at the head of our families—with the promise of the Lord that we will stand at the head of our own heavenly families.

Chapter 5

FATHER AS PRIESTHOOD BEARER

Children have unusual ways of reminding us of some important experiences that can be ours as a father/priesthood bearer.

One day our little son Brett was miserably sick. When I went into his room to check on him, he asked me, "Daddy, will you give me a prayer?" What he was asking for was a priesthood's healing blessing.

"Yes, Brett, Daddy will be glad to give you a blessing." And I laid my hands upon his head and commanded by the power of the priesthood—not of myself— that on the morrow he would be well. Then Brett settled down to sleep.

The next morning as we were assembling ourselves for family prayer, he came in. His older sister, Kristi, said, "I thought you were sick."

Brett replied as only a child with undaunted faith could, "Oh, didn't you know? Daddy blessed me. I have to be well."

Oh, the faith of a child!

A mother is blessed in bearing the child, in caring for its special needs, in nurturing its tender spirit. Through her, mortal birth is accomplished. Her rewards are understandably sweet. But what deep joy comes into the heart of the father who brings to his family members the gospel through the priesthood that he holds. Through it and its saving ordinances, they are born again spiritually.

What a system! What a marvelous plan that Heavenly Father has instituted for our development and joy and the blessing of those over whom we have stewardship!

Consider the many dividends that a father as a priesthood holder can bring to his family:

1. There is the benefit of physical contact (so often hard for a man to comfortably have with his children) as the father/priesthood bearer lays his hands upon the head of a loved one, as the two of them go down into the waters of baptism together, as they kneel side by side in prayer, as they embrace following the sacred moments in communion with Heavenly Father.

2. There is the commitment that surfaces anew in the father/priesthood bearer to be especially helpful to the person whom he has blessed. Having been an instrument of the Lord in a sacred ordinance, he is quickened to his own part in bringing to pass the fulfillment of that blessing.

3. There is the sobering sense of stewardship that comes when a father feels needed in such a potent way as described above. With such responsibility, he is likely to seek Heavenly Father earnestly in behalf of the loved one. And in the seeking, he looks to his own worthiness. He repents. He renews his own covenants. He is humbled and is therefore more usable by the Lord. The more receptive he is to the promptings of the Spirit, of course, the more choice and sacred is the experience for all concerned.

4. To the loved one being blessed, the father has added dimension, a strengthened image in his role of priesthood bearer. Here is security. Here is direction. Here is hope. Here is the one who counsels with the Lord for the benefit of his own loved ones. All will be well with the family headed by such a father.

The example of obedience and obeisance to God that a man shows under these circumstances, the faith he exhibits and the tenderness he expresses, all are examples of manhood at its most superb. Even when he is blessing others than his own family, the result is much the same. People are lifted and comforted by a brother who will step out of a work-a-day world and the pressures of the competitive life to follow prescribed procedures for the well-being of his brothers and sisters in the gospel.

At our house, even though it is a frequent and familiar practice, a father's blessing is not taken for granted. It is one of the first things the children think about when they have troubles—to have daddy use his special powers given by Heavenly Father to "make everything all right," as my little ones say.

I recall one time when Cory, age four, was having trouble sleeping through the nights. His dreams were so disturbing and recurring that he didn't want to go to sleep. Night after night he would ask me, "Daddy, bless me!" And I would go to his bedroom with him, lay my hands upon his head, and bless him that he would sleep peacefully and that all would be well with him that night. Often before my hands would leave his head, he would be fast asleep, now secure in the knowledge and comfortable in the faith that everything would be all right since his daddy, whose big hands had earlier played ball with Cory, had now laid those hands upon his head in a special ordinance and through the power of the priesthood of Heavenly Father—the Melchizedek Priesthood—had given him a blessing.

Can such comfort really be equaled any other way in the life of a child who can turn to his own father and be blessed specifically in time of need? It is then that even a child can understand and feel the Lord's goodness. When it has to do with God's will for us, we all can grow from taking another look at a principle or a procedure, at an ordinance or an opportunity so familiar to us. So it is with our priesthood. Only someone who is unaware of the true magnitude and power possible through the priesthood could be casual in performing such tasks, or through forgetfulness or self-consciousness deprive his loved ones of the fullest blessings God wants his children to have.

This is why each of us must know our role as a father/priesthood bearer.

Let us go back to Cory for a moment. He asked for the blessing. This is how he has been taught. But couldn't he have had a story read to him to lull him off to sleep? Or perhaps I could have lain down beside him until he dozed. Why not just his mother's comforting reminder,

"We are close by. You'll be fine!" Why a blessing? Why the hands placed upon his head and the words said?

Cory knew, as I know, that a priesthood blessing brings Heavenly Father into the situation—and that makes all the difference.

What is this priesthood to which we have been ordained?

What are our rights, privileges, obligations, and rewards in our capacity as a father/priesthood bearer?

How can we best be magnified in such a blessed privilege?

How can we most beautifully bless those within our realm of stewardship or others who may call upon us in need?

And what is the role of the Lord—he who is the giver of life, the one who calls us back again, our Redeemer, our ultimate comfort, the source of miracles great and small that change the quality of life for us— what is our relationship with him in this? He has said that he is bound when we do what he says. He has told us that if we will draw near unto him, he will draw near unto us. But what other action is triggered or generated by the actual procedures of the priesthood as prescribed by God and taught to us in the scriptures and by the prophets? All things that God has revealed or given to men may be acted upon by the power of the priesthood to bless people's lives. Sometimes revelation suggests counsel, chastisement, increased attention, fasting and prayer, pondering, and study, and sometimes the laying on of hands. The determining factor is whether the person requests a priesthood blessing by the laying on of hands.

We have been counseled over and over again in our priesthood meetings that if we brethren will be united in our priesthood, if we will act as one in carrying out the purposes of the Lord, there is absolutely nothing that can withstand this power. We have been reminded that such strength begins with the individual, and the individual is shaped in his home and then in church and elsewhere in his environment.

With such understanding, we are again awakened

to the critical importance of making our performance equal to the privilege and power that are ours.

This is why we must teach Cory and the others in our lives to have faith in God and to ask for priesthood blessings.

A man can be exalted only when he has—

1. Received the gospel,
2. Been ordained to the Melchizedek Priesthood,
3. Received the fulness of the priesthood as it comes to us in the temples of the Lord through the endowment and sealing ordinances, and
4. Lives faithfully and valiantly to the end.

And a man's family can only be exalted in the same way!

It is up to the head of each family to see to it that those who come under his stewardship are taught and blessed, that they are participants in the sacred ordinances of the Church, and that they, too, are valiant.

What is the priesthood, we might ask again?

It is the medium or channel through which our Father in heaven communicates light, gifts, and special intelligence necessary for spiritual and temporal salvation. Something we brethren too often fail to realize is that priesthood is not only the authority to represent God, but it is also the power that makes valid the ordinances the Lord has said are necessary for exaltation. We not only hold the keys to baptize and confirm, to bless and ordain our children, and to receive revelation concerning their well-being—we not only have these rights, but our Heavenly Father also expects us to use them. There will surely come a day when we will stand before the Lord to make an accounting of our stewardship.

Consider these enlightening thoughts on priesthood:

It [the priesthood] is nothing more nor less than the power of God delegated to man by which man can act in the earth for the salvation of the human family, in the name of the Father and the Son and the Holy Ghost, and act legitimately; not assuming that authority, not borrowing it from generations that are dead and gone, but authority that has been given in this day in which we

*live by ministering angels and spirits from above, direct
from the presence of Almighty God. . . . (Joseph F. Smith,
Gospel Doctrine, pp. 139-40.)*

*If anybody wants to know what the priesthood of
the Son of God is, it is the law by which the worlds are,
were, and will continue forever and ever. It is that
system which brings worlds into existence and peoples
them, gives them their revolutions—their days, weeks,
months, years, their seasons and times and by which
they are rolled up as a scroll, as it were, and go into a
higher state of existence. . . . The Priesthood is a perfect
system of government, of laws and ordinances, by which
we can be prepared to pass from one gate to another,
and from one sentinel to another, until we go into the
presence of our Father and God. (Brigham Young, Discourses of Brigham Young, p. 130.)*

*Every member of the church of Christ having
children is to bring them unto the elders before the
church, who are to lay their hands upon them in the
name of Jesus Christ, and bless them in his name. (D&C
20:70.)*

We who are counted among the elders of the
church and who have children are accountable to see to
it that our children are blessed in the name of Jesus
Christ. That means blessed with things that pertain to
Jesus Christ both temporal and spiritual.

*The power and authority of the higher, or Mel-
chizedek Priesthood, is to hold the keys of all the
spiritual blessings of the church—*
*To have the privilege of receiving the mysteries of
the kingdom of heaven, to have the heavens opened unto
them, to commune with the general assembly and church
of the Firstborn, and to enjoy the communion and
presence of God the Father, and Jesus the mediator of
the new covenant. (D&C 107:18-19.)*

The promise has been given us that we will receive
revelation, that the heavens will be open to us. What a
blessing for our family members to be so directed by a
father who is in touch with God!

For whoso is faithful unto the obtaining these two priesthoods of which I have spoken, and the magnifying their calling, are sanctified by the Spirit unto the renewing of their bodies.

They become the sons of Moses and of Aaron and the seed of Abraham, and the church and kingdom, and the elect of God.

And also all they who receive this priesthood receive me, saith the Lord. (D&C 84:33-35.)

No power or influence can or ought to be maintained by virtue of the priesthood, only by persuasion, by long-suffering, by gentleness and meekness, and by love unfeigned;

By kindness, and pure knowledge, which shall greatly enlarge the soul without hypocrisy, and without guile—

Reproving betimes with sharpness, when moved upon by the Holy Ghost; and then showing forth afterwards an increase of love toward him whom thou hast reproved, lest he esteem thee to be his enemy;

That he may know that thy faithfulness is stronger than the cords of death. (D&C 121:41-44.)

Yes, just as God's motive is love for all his actions, so to us as priesthood bearers, our motive must be love in order that we might serve. Is it beyond our understanding to grasp the significance of having our lives so lifted by priesthood service—leading our families into righteousness by inspiration from God—that our bodies would be renewed and our spirits sanctified? The company of the church on earth is filling with men who have made the decision to accept the priesthood, to receive this power from God, and to be magnified in it through keeping the commandments, striving for perfection, and serving those for whom they have special responsibility. It is not an assignment in life that can be delegated to anyone else. To be a father/priesthood bearer, to properly fill the role, brings blessings immeasurable to a man and his family.

But just as there are great rewards that come with the blessings, so are there penalties that come with disobedience.

Behold, there are many called, but few are chosen. And why are they not chosen?

Because their hearts are set so much upon the things of this world, and aspire to the honors of men, that they do not learn this one lesson—

That the rights of the priesthood are inseparably connected with the powers of heaven, and that the powers of heaven cannot be controlled nor handled only upon the principles of righteousness.

That they may be conferred upon us, it is true; but when we undertake to cover our sins, or to gratify our pride, our vain ambition, or to exercise control or dominion or compulsion upon the souls of the children of men, in any degree of unrighteousness, behold, the heavens withdraw themselves; the Spirit of the Lord is grieved; and when it is withdrawn, Amen to the priesthood or the authority of that man. (D&C 121:34-37.)

Again, let us consider the case of Cory and his bad dreams. The blessing that put into play the powers of God unto the peace of this little boy's soul can be put into play as the problems and pressures of life become even more critical with the passing years. Multiply Cory by each growing child. Add a wife with her own needs and the constant demands upon her as mother, homemaker, church worker, and perhaps, on occasion, developing her own self outside the home and church. How greatly a father is needed who will live close to the Lord so that he can be a power and source of good in blessing and directing these loved ones.

There are two key questions to consider. First, am I an interested and striving (though imperfect) priesthood holder? Second, how and when do I use this privilege for the benefit of my wife and children?

As to the first question, we know and the Lord knows when we are being prayerful and growing in the gospel, when we are paying a full tithing, keeping ourselves unspotted from the world, keeping the Sabbath day holy, being honest in all our dealings, living an exemplary life in love and patience and caring so that relationships between the father/priesthood bearer and family members are close. The Spirit of the Lord will rest upon such a man as he tries, and he will wax strong and grow in wisdom, power, and confidence before the Lord and in his assignment as head of a family. He will become more effective because all things are possible through Jesus Christ whom he has chosen to follow. The priesthood is an appendage to Jesus Christ, and our power is brought to bear only as we receive strength from the Lord. We ourselves are weak, but with God's help we can do all things.

> *Yea, I know that I am nothing; as to my strength I am weak; therefore I will not boast of myself, but I will boast of my God, for in his strength I can do all things; yea, behold, many mighty miracles we have wrought in this land, for which we will praise his name forever."* (*Alma 26:12.*)

The second question concerning when we should exercise priesthood rights is clearly answered in priesthood meetings and manuals, in church publications, and in the scriptures. When a man truly accepts the responsibility of being the presiding authority in his home, is in tune with the Lord, and is responsive to the Spirit, he knows when he is to give the blessing and what he is to say. This would be in addition to those times when a bishop, stake president, or General Authority might call upon the father/priesthood bearer to assist in a special priesthood act, such as an ordination, baptism, confirmation, or setting apart, as well as those times when a family member requests a special blessing.

In-tune-ness lets a father/priesthood bearer be responsive to the suggestions of the mother/wife whose role puts her in touch with the needs of the children. He also senses by the Spirit when a blessing by the laying on of hands is needed, or when, instead, the matter should be handled through counsel and/or fasting and prayer on the part of the individual.

There is no question that God desires the salvation and well-being, spiritually and temporally, of all his children. He has counseled us to pray over our "flocks and our fields" as well as to pray for spiritual growth and protection from the adversary. He uses his servants on earth to bring good into the lives of his children, and a father/priesthood bearer has unique and marvelous ways of assisting.

Some appropriate occasions for a laying-on-of-the-hands priesthood blessing would be in times of sickness or extreme distress, before a student in the family starts school, a mission, a marriage, military service, or other pressing assignment or responsibility. I know of more than one instance when trouble between a husband and wife was finally resolved when the wife at last went to her own husband/priesthood bearer (at the reminder of a church priesthood leader) for such a blessing. Oh, the unity and the quality of heavenliness that can come into a marriage and into a family, permeating the home to the point where others feel its warmth, when the gospel is lived and the priesthood blessings are claimed!

Life is a struggle as well as a beautiful adventure. But we need all the help we can get to return to the presence of our Heavenly Father, organized as families and dwelling together in peace and love. The mortal world is an extremely urgent force in our daily existence, and sometimes we forget to focus on the long-range blessings. But the Lord has not left us wanting here on earth. He has provided—

1. The priesthood and all that it means—its eternal nature from before the world was, through Adam, down through the generations of prophets to each individual priesthood bearer. It is for us fathers to use this precious privilege (with what knowledge we now have of its workings) and to continue to grow in commitment and effectiveness.

2. Gospel principles to help us perfect ourselves and become more like him.

3. The institution of the Church and its variety of helps and instructions, motivations, and involvements to keep us growing in the right direction.

4. Opportunities for us to suffer, to taste the bitter and the sweet, to be challenged, tested, and tried, that we might be honed and humbled unto the magnifying of our spiritual selves. When we use our special powers to

directly offer relief in the name of Jesus Christ, unity and love are the blessed results.

To the person in the family home who is *not* the father but is the priesthood bearer, let the challenge to take hold of this privilege be his as well. He can bless the family as far as his priesthood permits. He can call the family to prayer, teach the principle of the fast, remind the family of the instructions of the prophets, hold family home evening, and look to the personal resources and needs of the family with inspiration from the Lord. He can be the example and friend to his own father if the father does not hold the priesthood, and in love can help him take his place as head of the family and encourage his rightful opportunity to ready himself for the full role of father/priesthood bearer.

This is the Lord's plan for all his spirit children. It is our blessing to follow his plan for us. When a child says, "Daddy, give me a blessing," may we be ready to arise to the occasion.

Chapter 6

FATHER AS LEADER

Have you ever walked through a car lot, fingered a fender, kicked a tire, and turned to find your boy imitating you exactly—not even knowing why he's doing what he's doing? I have. It is sobering.

One day I had my two young sons in tow on a tour of used cars and did just that—kicked a tire. Brett, age five, came along behind me and was just withdrawing his toe from a kick when Cory, age three, tested that tire in the identical manner.

At first I laughed. Then I got a feeling of panic as I realized how the game of follow-the-leader is very real in life. And it has to do with more than kicking tires.

We have scripture reading time at our house, and everyone has been taught to mark his or her personal copy of the Book of Mormon. Cory, too young to read or write, had been content to watch or look at the pictures in his illustrated version while we all enthusiastically went about our study time together. Then there came a day—and this is what a father never can judge exactly—when Cory wanted to be part of the action. He suddenly left the group, raced to his coloring box, and came back with a red crayon to start marking up his book, too. I felt like some kind of wonderful father that day. All the early struggles of rounding up the troops for scripture time was now worth it—somebody did it because he really wanted to!

I found myself thinking of all kinds of great things I could lead the children into. I could lead them into picking up their clothes, cleaning the garage, helping mother without being asked, showing respect for their brothers and sisters and mother, being loyal to each other, honoring the priesthood of a brother when daddy wasn't around, supporting the bishop, going to the polls to vote, obeying the law, observing the Sabbath, respecting the property of others, not criticizing church leaders, programs, principles, taking a stand against evil in whatever form, using clean language, controlling the disposition, protecting health, developing talents, improving the mind, having courage to stand alone or to defend. Oh, I could lead these loved ones of mine right into the celestial kingdom in my weakness but strengthened by the Lord.

And so, father, may each of you be a leader you'd like to follow.

The Savior has shown us a critical clue to success in leadership. Said he, "Therefore, what manner of men ought ye to be? Verily I say unto you, even as I am." (3 Nephi 27:27.) A prerequisite to good leadership is to know what manner of being Christ really was, to gain a testimony of him and a commitment to follow his teachings. There is no more important knowledge one can gain in the world than this. It will change one's own life and will affect the lives of those who follow him. We must come to know the Savior and to follow him. Then those who follow us are more likely to grow up to follow him. How blessed they'll be!

Elder Marion D. Hanks tells the story of the man who approached him on Temple Square in Salt Lake City and asked how one got inside the temple. When Elder Hanks began talking to him as if he were one of the many tourists who frequently ask that question, the man protested and explained that he was already a Mormon; he was asking only because his wife had dragged him to the square and wanted to know for herself.

As the details of the man's story unfolded, it was disturbing to realize how far-reaching are the effects of a priesthood leader's behavior and another's reaction to such behavior. It seems that when he had been a young man, he had been banished from church by a bishop's counselor for making a disturbance in Sunday School class. As he was being escorted angrily to the door

43

someone objected, but the counselor answered, "Aw, let him go. He is just one kid!"

Yes, that boy went, never to return. He married three times and had fifty-four descendants. Fifty-four people not members of the Church because one priesthood leader had chosen to throw a boy out of meeting instead of working with him to solve problems as a leader in the Lord's church ought to do!

What import a leader has in the lives of his family members and others over whom he has authority to direct, guide, lead.

Facing up to the fact that we'll be followed wherever we go—whether we are leading or simply lumbering along ourself—sobers a member of the priesthood. Our imperfections and shortcomings begin to emerge upon the mind in bold relief. Maybe we didn't find the gospel until lately. Maybe our own father let us down in some important ways, led us along some paths we shouldn't have traveled. Perhaps our choices haven't all been wise ones. We may even have reaped a whirlwind or two and developed some foolish habits. Well, the principle of repentance is one of the Lord's best blessings. Repent. Turn around. Change. Stop. Start over.

Remember, we are agents to ourselves. We are grown men. We can still choose to act instead of react. We can change. We don't go charging across the barrier reading "bridge out" just because we didn't see the sign. As soon as we get the message, we must respond or be a loser. In England, where the traffic moves in the opposite direction from what we in America are used to, one doesn't quibble over how or why not wait until he remembers to change long-established habits of traffic procedures. He changes, now! People do remember at once to deal with the traffic on a different basis from home. They just do. There's so much at stake.

Too often our problem in self-change is that we don't get the vision of what the traffic pattern really is, or we don't watch for the warning signs and thus drive right on through to destruction. At best we take detours that may delay our trip but will ultimately bring us great happiness.

Even the Lord doesn't expect our perfection all at once. Just as we expect his forgiveness, his continued blessing, and his patience with us, so we must do the same for those who follow us. Line upon line, strength upon strength we grow—we follow, we lead, and others follow us similarly.

Never underestimate the power of the priesthood. Let's acknowledge our own amazing power through the Lord and determine to grow into it magnificently. When President Joseph Fielding Smith died and Elder Harold B. Lee became the prophet and president of the Church, he told how unprepared he felt, how much growing he had to do, how dependent he was upon the Lord.

When Wilhelmina, the young woman who became queen of the Netherlands upon her father's death, stood on the palace balcony to greet the thousands of cheering subjects below, she was overwhelmed. She turned to her widowed mother and remarked, "Do all of these belong to me?" "No," replied the wise mother, "but you belong to all of them." Therein lies a key to good leadership. We should admit to the power we have to influence and serve, and then rise to the occasion.

Christ is our leader. The beautiful example he set for us ought to be a part of our own procedure in dealing with those whom we are appointed to lead.

Remember the time of the passover, which the disciples had been celebrating in the customary way with a special feast. It was to be the last supper before Christ's crucifixion, and he, the superb example, was teaching the most important principle of all in helping others along the path in life. The scripture reads:

He riseth from supper, and laid aside his garments; and took a towel, and girded himself.

After that he poureth water into a bason, and began to wash the disciples' feet, and to wipe them with the towel wherewith he was girded. . . .

. . . He said unto them, Know ye what I have done to you?

Ye call me Master and Lord: and ye say well; for so I am.

If I then, your Lord and Master, have washed your feet; ye also ought to wash one another's feet.

For I have given you an example, that ye should do as I have done to you. . . . (John 13:4-5, 13-15.)

Christ went on to explain that he who would be chief should be the servant of all. Then he said another very significant thing: "If ye know these things, happy are ye if ye do them." (John 13:17.)

We may not be perfect nor have full knowledge of all things yet, but what good we do know, we should do. Then we will be happy, for the Lord has so promised.

We are all thankful for the teachers and leaders who have helped us and our loved ones over life's hurdles to greater understanding and more effective performance. Surely there are those grateful for our part in their lives, too. Yet we can never be sure that someone else will be there and will have the special inspiration from God that can make a difference with our child. It is our assignment. If not us, then who can be counted upon to do it as it ought to be done for this wonderful loved one of ours?

If the leader trumps uncertainly or if he comes and goes in variable strengths and showings of concern, what of the troops that wait to follow? A wonderful story is told of Civil War days that should lend important perspective on this subject. At a place known as Missionary Ridge on the outskirts of Chattanooga, Tennessee, the numerically superior Southern troops had dug in to protect the ridge against a Northern attack. These defenders were seemingly invulnerable in their position and with their fortifications, yet they lost the hill to the Northern forces. Why? Because they were so isolated from one another in their own spots that they lost touch with one another. They couldn't hear or see their leader in the ruckus, but the enemy was plainly in sight and coming toward them. Each man entrenched on the ridge felt that he was alone with the enemy, and so they panicked; after some of them surrendered, others followed suit.

We must be ready to lead, to be followed. We must

be in sight and certain of our course, with constant, firm directions to those whom we lead. Otherwise, it is highly possible in today's battles that some of those whom we love will surrender in confusion and aloneness and uncertainty.

Three factors a father must consider when he leads out in life are timing, patience, and awareness. One can never be exactly sure just when leadership will be followed, when what we are doing will be picked up by others. It is possible, too, for us to become weary of well-doing and to give up too soon on a training procedure just before a child might respond. Leading that horse to the water truly doesn't insure its immediate drinking from the well, but it is a sure thing that if we don't get him to the well at all, he'll be unable to quench his thirst when he's ready to.

Leadership, priesthood, and fatherhood in the church of Jesus Christ are synonomous. The absolutely awesome station in life in which we find ourselves as head of the home would seem to require our own readiness to learn how to lead out better. We fathers have been brought to the well on countless occasions. Let us hope and pray that we are at last ready to drink from the truths of the gospel. We need all the help we can get. There is so much to lose if we don't arise to this occasion. We will lose those very homes and loved ones to whom we could have laid claim.

How great are the rewards in a home where the mother takes pleasure in her children, where the father leads out in devotion, and where the children in turn honor their parents with their hearts. This is the sum and core of God's plan—of motherhood, priesthood, and the system of childhood in a parental encirclement. Home is the center of the gospel, and it should be the place we want to be more than any other. It is the reason for going elsewhere at all—that we might come back to enrich those within.

President David O. McKay once said:

The poorest shack where love prevails over a united family is of far greater value to God and future humanity than other riches. In such a home God can work miracles, and will work miracles. Pure hearts in a pure home are always in whispering distance of heaven.

Let us ever remember, brethren, that God's miracles are worked through us as his instruments. We must be in tune. We must be receptive, humble, striving, believing. We must accept our privilege and begin wherever we are at this moment to be magnified in precious opportunities to bless and guide our families.

There once was a pharaoh who consulted with the great teacher named Euripedes on the matter of improving himself. He wanted to be taught geometry so his mind would be disciplined. After things had been going along nicely for a time, the pharaoh suddenly became impatient and said to Euripedes, "Isn't there an easier way to learn geometry than going through all this?"

"This is the only way," answered Euripedes.

"But I am Pharaoh!"

"Aye, sire," was the reply, "but there is no royal road to geometry!"

There is no royal road for fathers in becoming like unto their Heavenly Father. The Lord has taught us that the way is straight and narrow and requires constancy, endurance, and much improving of the mind and soul.

Here's a checklist to consider, in evaluating ourselves as fathers.

1. *Do I keep all the commandments of God as I understand them?*
2. *Am I increasing my knowledge and understanding through study and prayer?*
3. *Am I nourishing my family spiritually?*
4. *Do I pray alone for guidance; with my wife in good spirit and sincerity daily; with my children when either I or they feel the need; with my family all together as counseled by God and his prophets?*
5. *Am I setting and achieving goals personally? with my wife? Are we doing this as a family?*
6. *Do we hold family prayer daily, family home evening regularly, and family councils to deal with problems and opportunities?*

7. How are things at home, really? Do I feel a part or apart?

8. Am I followed when I lead? Are my family members confused, obedient, disgruntled, growing, resentful, respectful—which, and when?

9. Is there a good spirit in our family? Is our haven a whisper from heaven?

10. Are my family members involved in church opportunities, loyal to church standards and leaders, converted to Christ, and reaching higher?

11. Am I willing to listen to God, to my wife, to my children, to my bishop, to my priesthood file leader, and to the president of the Church?

12. Do I consider my priesthood assignments in the Church to be a privilege or as jobs to "get done"?

13. Have I ever exercised "unrighteous dominion" instead of gentle persuasion? Do I need to change my attitude and approach?

14. Am I ready to make my report on my stewardship before God?

15. Have I seriously considered the alternatives to the road the Lord has told us to travel? Do I really understand what is at stake if I fail as a father, husband, leader in our home?

16. Am I selfish? self-oriented? self-seeking? self-pitying? restless? a target with whom the adversary could make some headway?

17. Is my example a worthy one? Are my appearance, demeanor, language, and attitude what my children would expect to find in a true follower of Christ?

18. Do I give praise or expect it?

19. Do I delegate or dictate—ask to help or to be helped?

20. Am I repentant? sincere? striving?

21. Do I accept the privilege of fatherhood and stewardship and leadership with thankfulness before God? before those beloved family members assigned to me?

And now, brethren, the big question: Do I love my family?

The Lord has taught us that the first and great commandment is to love God the Father and Jesus Christ, whom he sent to redeem, teach, and bless us. Secondly, we are to love others as ourselves. A leader without true concern (which brings about righteous service) is a leader without followership. Let's look into our own experiences as a follower to see the truth in that statement. Oh, the wisdom in remembering the counsel and commandment to love each other as Christ has loved us!

Such love helps us surmount the problems, endure in grace the hardships of life, and enjoy to the maximum the blessings of eternal family life. Honestly, now, father/leader, is there any other more rewarding or satisfying or superior way to live than to say to your family, "Follow me as I follow Christ"?

Chapter 7

FATHER
AS TEACHER

One day I visited the Junior Sunday School in our ward. The behavior of one little boy was particularly troublesome. In desperation the teacher finally threatened, "Larry, if you don't settle down and be good, I'm going to take you upstairs to your dad." "Won't do you any good," the child sulked in return, suddenly quiet. "My dad isn't up there to take me to." Week after week the little fellow had been dropped off at church, I discovered later, and left while his father went off to the golf course or to make rounds at the hospital and his mother slept in. What was this little boy being taught at home?

Family home evenings aren't always perfect at our house. We try—sometimes harder than other times. Sometimes the best lessons come in unexpected ways. I recall hearing of a father who was trying to teach a discussion on love for one another in his family. He had shown pictures of happy families doing different things in many different cultural settings so his children would get a broadened view of the families in Heavenly Father's larger family, and he thought the lesson was going along fine. Everyone seemed interested in black families, Oriental families, tribal families, and Swiss families—everyone, that is, except little Janie, whose attention simply got lost in the shuffle of visual aids. Families were all the same to her. So she began to kick her foot against the chair and play with the cooing lovebirds the father had used to illustrate love in the families among God's creatures. Once she'd figured out how to make those birds coo-coo and tweet-tweet at each other, she repeated the process over and over. Father wanted to get the lesson finished and the children into their mother's hands for bed so he could settle down to his own projects, so he forged on with his lesson. However, Jane persisted in her annoying kicks and tricks. Finally, in great impatience, he lashed out at her, "Janie! Stop that at once! Good grief, how much do you think I can stand?" Janie settled down. Big ogre daddy had spoken.

The next day he went to Janie's room to call her to the table for dinner and overheard her saying to her doll in a heartbreaking imitation of his outburst the night before, "Good grief, Dolly! Stop that at once! How much do you think I can stand?" Three-year-olds have an agonizing way of learning what we had no intention of teaching them.

What kind of teaching is going on at our house?

What are our children learning from us?

Do we love our family enough to repent and change our ways if necessary, in order to be a better model for them?

You see, it isn't so much what we teach as what they learn from us. What we are speaks so loudly that they can't hear a word we say. I have found that children whose understanding is still limited or an adult who is not fully converted to the gospel of Jesus Christ will perform at the level of the environment in which they associate. If the father lives on a telestial level, the children often do also until some other better influence may at last reach them. This is frighteningly true. When a father sits through that heart-tugging time while his wife delivers a newborn son, he vows to improve himself, to somehow be worthy of the privilege of parenting. To a priesthood bearer with eternal stewardship over these spirits entrusted to him, this is an even more acute experience.

One man made a telling statement when he was named Father of the Year:

If it were in my power to bestow on the youth of the land one single quality, . . . I would choose integrity. If one day my children and grandchildren say to one another, "He taught us to value integrity," I shall be content. . . . If your children are to have integrity, they must find it in the home and in you. (Joseph Welch.)

How is the quality of integrity passed on to the children in our homes? How is the quality of honesty or of obedience to the Lord's commandments impressed upon them? How does a child learn graciousness, sensitivity to spiritual promptings, and how to cope effectively with temptation or adversity?

In Proverbs we are told, "Train up a child in the way he should go: and when he is old, he will not depart from it." (Proverbs 22:6.) And in the Doctrine and Covenants the Lord counsels:

And again, inasmuch as parents have children in Zion, or in any of her stakes which are organized, that teach them not to understand the doctrine of repentance, faith in Christ the Son of the living God, and of baptism and the gift of the Holy Ghost by the laying on of the hands, when eight years old, the sin be upon the heads of the parents. (D&C 68:25.)

As we study the word of the Lord, there is little question that we are to formally teach and deliberately instruct our children in principles and practices of righteousness. However, we must practice what we preach, because they may learn something other than the lesson we had in mind.

God gives us a mighty clue to effective teaching when he says, "And these words, which I command thee this day, shall be in thine heart: And thou shalt teach them diligently unto thy children, and shalt talk of them when thou sittest in thine house, and when thou walkest by the way, and when thou liest down, and when thou risest up." (Deuteronomy 6:6-7.) The poetry of that counsel should not be permitted to hide the incredible wisdom of it. The best teaching comes in daily behavior—at all hours and in all the homely happenings. We must live, breathe, explain, describe, and affirm the truths at all times. Every moment can be a teaching moment.

Someone has humorously but truthfully declared:

Parents may tell
But never teach
Unless they practice
What they preach.

How true that is! The Lord said, "And also trust no one to be your teacher nor your minister, except he be a man of God, walking in his ways and keeping his commandments." (Mosiah 23:14.) What we are trying to become in our life is what will mark the success of our effort in helping our children lift their lives.

Being an effective teacher of the truths of life does not mean that a father needs a graduate degree in education. This is too narrow a connotation for the grand promises of the Lord to his sons who will be magnified in their priesthood through faithfulness. In the good intentions of their hearts for the benefit of others, performance will surmount natural ability. When one lives to merit the gifts thereof, the Holy Ghost can enlighten and enliven, instruct and bear witness of, and call to mind hidden truths that no college degree could ever reveal to man and that no one can truly teach except by the power of the Holy Ghost.

Some of us are getting a late start. New members, newly activated, and freshly awakened fathers often have children who have grown up without abundant gospel teachings. Repentance is a redeeming principle. A father who has not been active in the Church can bear his testimony that he regrets not knowing the truths sooner. He can let his family know that he cares about their lives and their learnings, and that as he prayerfully seeks knowledge and the guidance of the Spirit, he will try to be of help to those for whom he is responsible, those whom he loves above all else on earth.

Enthusiasm literally means inspired by God, or God in us. Positive, hopeful, undaunted, the converted father is a contagious teacher. He acts as he thinks. "I care." "I'm learning." "I want to share some additional truths I've discovered with you." "Come follow me, as I follow the Savior."

The Church of Jesus Christ of Latter-day Saints has excellent aids for disseminating the truth: publications, pamphlets, programs, and people who are well-meaning, unselfish, inspired models. Father and mother do not stand alone in the task of bringing to pass the immortality and eternal life of their own posterity.

Fathers in this role as priesthood bearers trying to teach the gospel to their families might ask themselves some very searching questions. Pondering meditation is the Lord's way of getting through to us because we are in a listening, receiving frame of mind. Consider:

1. *How do I feel about each one in my family—each individual?*
2. *What have I learned in life? What do I want them to know?*
3. *What do I think they need to know?*
4. *What would have helped me in my life if I'd known this sooner?*
5. *What methods can I use to help my loved ones change, improve, grow, repent, get involved, get motivated in the gospel of Jesus Christ?*
6. *Why do I want them to know these things?*
7. *What will I do about it if they refuse to listen and act?*
8. *What kind of model or example am I of the things I am teaching?*
9. *Am I continuing to grow? Am I increasing in humility, teachableness?*
10. *Am I living by the principles I've come to understand?*

Tolstoy told the tale of the ruler who wanted to be superior in his assignment, so he went up into the hills alone and consulted the wise old hermit who had time to meditate on important things. The ruler wanted to know whom to give his attention to and what course of action to follow. The wise hermit replied that the ruler should begin now, while he had the chance; that he should do good; and that he should begin with those closest around him. The rest would take care of itself.

Beginning with what we know, we teach to our children in an attitude of humility and conviction. When Alma returned from his missionary journey to the land of the apostate Zoramites, he was discouraged and his heart was exceeding sorrowful. Therefore, he caused that his sons should be gathered together, that he might give unto each one of them his charge "concerning the things pertaining unto righteousness." (Alma 35:16.)

What do we teach our children?

We teach that God lives.

We acknowledge Christ as our Redeemer in our heart, mind, and life, and urge our loved ones to do the same, through their free agency.

We teach and witness that the gospel is the only way to eternal peace and joy. The sooner we learn the lessons, the sooner our joy will come.

We teach that the institution of The Church of Jesus Christ of Latter-day Saints is the Lord's organization on earth where the fulness of his truths and guidelines for life and saving ordinances can be found.

We teach the fruits of the gospel, proof that the Church is true and that people are happier and more blessed within its fold.

We teach that God the Father and Jesus Christ appeared to the Prophet Joseph Smith in our time and that he was an appointed prophet of God.

We teach how the Book of Mormon came to be, that it is valid, and that it contains wisdom for our own lives today.

We teach that we have a living prophet of God today through whom the Lord still reveals his will for us.

We teach the validity and power and authority of the priesthood; its blessing in our lives and our responsibility to use it in behalf of others; and that the priesthood can exist without the church, but the church cannot function without the priesthood.

We teach principles, ordinances, and specific commandments of God. We teach theology, but we also testify of the rewards of it. Faith, repentance, forgiveness, baptism, prayer, love—oh, we need to teach and testify of these things!

We teach by precept and example to honor authority and law, to have reverence for the earth and the fulness thereof, to love our neighbors and do unto them as we would enjoy being treated ourselves.

We teach attitudes that help us cope with adversity, endure in equanimity, accept with patience, withstand temptation, and defend righteousness.

We teach peace and the blessedness of being peacemakers instead of problem people.

We teach, as King Benjamin taught through the inspiration of God, that we must walk in the ways of truth and soberness, to love one another, and to serve one another.

And we teach how to know for ourselves all that the Lord wants us to know as truth. (See Moroni 10.)

A story is used in educational circles that I believe in because, as a father and a university lecturer, I've found the principle of it to be true.

An educational leader engaged a number of teachers in the primary grades to take on the challenge of becoming special friends to a certain group of children who were not making it in the grade school curriculum and activities. The teachers weren't special experts in this field, just good teachers. The children had no apparent reason for being underachievers. They weren't mentally retarded, emotionally disturbed, nor temporally deprived; but they were on their way to certain more serious problems. The project was conducted without telling the children about it at all. When the time limit for the challenge was over, the success report was overwhelming. The children were all achieving! Each one loved and wanted to please his "friend," his special teacher.

Because we care about our own children, we must become their special friend. As we come to love Christ, the Master Teacher, and as we come under his influence, we too move ahead. John Milton said, "The end of all learning is to know God, and out of that learning to love and imitate him." As our children come to recognize in us someone who expects the best in them and who will love them always, regardless of what may happen, they will live better lives.

Surely it can be said that as fathers we are always

teaching. For lifting or lowering a life, everything we think, say, support, criticize, do, or forget to do—everything we are—can be learned by our children. Therefore, the greatest service we can perform in life is to put before them the finest example of ourself.

"And now the Spirit of the Lord doth say unto me: Command thy children to do good, lest they lead away the hearts of many people to destruction; therefore I command you, my son, in the fear of God, that ye refrain from your iniquities." (Alma 39:12.)

The commandment is ours to teach by precept and by example, through preparation and through the Spirit. Will our children say, as Enos said, "Behold, it came to pass that I, Enos, knowing my father that he was a just man—for he taught me in his language, and also in the nurture and admonition of the Lord—and blessed be the name of my God for it." (Enos 1.)

Fathers, let us remember that someone is learning something from us. What is that we are teaching?

Chapter 8

**FATHER
AS FRIEND**

A profound statement is found in the book of Proverbs (17:17): "A friend loveth at all times." A father who would be a friend to his family and feels he has earned their friendship in return must love at all times. That means when the fender is crumpled, when the chores aren't done on time, when orders are not followed, when the phone is busy and the household confusion is great. It suggests, fathers, that those whom we are to love and from whom we are to find love eternally, we must befriend. We must learn to like them as well as love them.

One of the most impressive reports about fathers is a report made some time ago in an Indianapolis school district. It seems that the fathers in that district were not supporting PTA. Sound familiar? One teacher who counted a father's influence as most important and wanted to lure fathers to a PTA meeting where such matters could be brought to the attention assigned the children to write essays about "What I Like About Daddy." These essays would be read out loud—anonymously—in the meeting. The fathers, of course, came. They came in their small cars, their campers, their super specials. They came in clothes reflecting their daily work, their life-style and their personal taste. They came with some apprehension as well. What would these children have to say about their fathers?

The letters were picked at random and all were quite similar. Each youngster listed what he liked about his father, from the fact that he had built a doll house to helping fatten a pig to sell. Out of 326 school children, the sum expression of dad was that he was a friend—he played with them, helped them, spent time with them doing the things they liked or needed. Not one mentioned the kind of car dad drove, what he did for work, the size of the house he'd provided for them, the way he looked.

Each father came to that meeting with his own opinion of himself and an image of his contribution to his child's life. Each went away knowing for certain that he was important to his child in relation to the time he spent doing the things his child liked.

When a man has the stewardship to help to bring to pass the immortality and eternal life of his family, he had better administer his jurisdiction in such a way as to reach them. How else can this goal of eternal life be met? Friends can reach and touch. Strangers can't accomplish the same things as a good and trusted friend.

The counsel oft-given that parents should know where their children are is indeed valid. How much better if the parent is with the child, if the hours outside of school, church, work are spent at home with the company of true friends like parents, who have the largest imaginable stake in their children's well-being. We need to keep our minds on our children. We need to let our thoughts and prayers go out with them and our hearts and attention be upon them when they come home.

I will never forget when this truth became firmly implanted in my mind. One night I had arrived home tired, worn-out, and in need of some relaxation. I promptly found the evening newspaper, slipped off my shoes, propped my feet up on my desk, and began to read. It wasn't long before my son Brett arrived, pleading, "Daddy, please let's make an airplane now."

Like a tired father, I replied, "Brett, can't you see I'm tired? I have had a hard day. Leave me alone for awhile."

He pleaded again, "Come on, Dad. It will only take a minute."

"Oh, Brett, we can do that later today. I want to rest. You go on—we'll work on it later."

Then, as I glanced up from my paper, I noticed the saddened face of one of my most priceless relationships—my son—as he walked away.

I wadded up the newspaper, threw it in the garbage, and ran after him, crying, "Wait, Brett! We can do it now. Daddy's got time. Daddy's got time."

That is when I realized that when I walk in the door of my home, I am father, servant, and friend of all.

One man admits to solving many of his family problems by leaving his briefcase at the office, because when he is home he wants to *be* home, to be available to his children. The briefcase in hand had been a signal to the family that dad had more important things to do. Perhaps the inspiration of this idea isn't always readily applicable, but it is a worthy goal, and that is better than no goal at all in finding ways to make every night a friendly gathering in our homes.

Interviews with children who are in trouble with the law or with school officials, or who are at odds with life and suffering some type of emotional problem, indicate that a strong friend in a father could often make a difference. It is how father acts and not where he is sitting that makes the difference. Children are sensitive to authenticity, and respect cannot be demanded. Neither can friendship. A family with a purposeful father whom each child likes is more apt to follow his counsel.

The scriptures have given us excellent insight into this matter:

And, ye fathers, provoke not your children to wrath: but bring them up in the nurture and admonition of the Lord. (Ephesians 6:4.)

Fathers, provoke not your children to anger, lest they be discouraged. (Colossians 3:21.)

Therefore, renounce war and proclaim peace, and seek diligently to turn the hearts of the children to their fathers, and the hearts of the fathers to the children. (D&C 98:16.)

Perhaps in too many instances we have considered that last quotation only in terms of doing our genealogy. Let us consider it here as vital that those who yet live with us as part of our own family circle need our heart—all of it—as we come together in love to worship, serve

God, struggle with the daily problems of life, and strive to keep God's commandments.

A well-meaning, conscientious, but pressured father who was presiding over a mission had an experience that we could all benefit from. He said that one night he asked his son to do something a second time and then a third time, but the boy just ignored him. Finally the father became annoyed and raised his voice, saying, "What is your problem? Can't you hear me? I said to turn off the light!"

The son just looked at his father for a moment and then lowered his head.

"Well?" asked the father, trying to control his temper.

"Well, Dad," replied the boy at last, "it's just that I've had it with your treating me like a second-class citizen—as if I were a robot and not a person. I've noticed that you don't treat the missionaries this way. You jolly them up. You listen when they say something. You always say 'Please' when you ask them to do something. You talk to them man-to-man instead of talking down like you do to me. That's what's the matter."

The father was thoroughly shaken by what he had just heard. He sent a prayer heavenward and then moved to his son and put his arm around him and apologized. As the father humbly admitted the error of his ways before his son, the boy warmed toward his father, and it was the starting point for a better turn in their relationship. If we would be a friend to our children, we need to think about them as being God's children, too; as being persons, not inanimate objects or creatures just to be at our beck and call.

A story is told that illustrates the importance of persisting in our efforts to show forth love to our children. As we keep trying, we will grow in skill and effectiveness in becoming friends with these precious people in our life. This is the story of a father who really loved his son and dared to say so:

Throughout my life as I grew up as a boy, my father and I had many serious arguments. One day, when I was seventeen, we had a particularly violent one. I said to him, "This is the straw that breaks the camel's back. I'm leaving, and I will never return." So saying, I went to the house and packed a bag. My mother begged me to stay, but I was too mad and upset to listen. I left her crying at the doorway.

As I left the yard and was about to pass through the gate, I heard my father call to me.

"Frank," he said, "I know that a large share of the blame for your leaving rests with me. For this I am deeply sorry. But I want you to know that if you should ever wish to return to our home, you'll always be welcome. And I'll try to be a better father to you. Finally, I want you to know that I'll always love you."

I said nothing, but went to the bus station and bought a ticket to a hundred miles from nowhere. But as I sat in the bus watching the miles go by I began to think about the words of my father. I began to realize how much maturity, how much goodness, how much love it had required for him to do what he had done. He had apologized. He had invited me back and he left the words ringing in my ears: "I love you."

It was then that I realized that the next move was up to me. I knew that the only way I could ever find peace with myself was to demonstrate to him the same kind of maturity, goodness and love that he had demonstrated toward me.

I got off the bus. I bought a return ticket to my home and went back. I arrived just shortly before midnight. I entered the house and turned on the light. There in our rocking chair sat my father, his head in his hands. As he looked up and saw me, he rose from the chair and we rushed into each other's arms.

One recognizes the elements of the prodigal son in this story, with a father rushing forth to meet his son. Isn't it so with us and our Heavenly Father? He is our friend. He forgives us our sins. He is available to us. When we draw near to him, he draws near to us. We can unveil ourselves before him, reveal unto him our hearts, and admit to him our failings and our needs. And always, the outpouring comes. Shouldn't we follow this sublime example with our own children?

Do you recall these words from the Sermon on the Mount:

. . . what man is there of you, whom if his son ask bread, will he give him a stone?

Or if he ask a fish, will he give him a serpent?

If ye then, being evil, know how to give good gifts unto your children, how much more shall your Father which is in heaven give good things to them that ask him?

Therefore all things whatsoever ye would that men should do to you, do ye even so to them: for this is the law and the prophets. (Matthew 7:9-12.)

Fathers, our own children are waiting for just such a friend as us—a friend who loveth at all times.

Chapter 9

FATHER
AS PROVIDER

Can you remember your first baseball mitt? I remember mine. I used to look at it in Bennett's window on West Center Street in Provo, Utah. How I wanted that glove! Each Saturday I'd go down, try it on, and think, "Eight more weeks of mowing lawns and you belong to me." Then it was seven, five, two weeks. Finally, it was mine. I mean, *really* mine.

My father had died a few years before, and with the money he had left us, mom could have bought me that glove. It would have been easier for her to lay out the cash than to put up with my constant enthusiasm for getting the mitt. But we had had something in addition to a bit of money from dad—we had had his training of us while he lived. We had time enough with him for him to have taught me how to mow a lawn; time for him to have taught me the dignity of work and the meaning of earning my own way. The influence of those lessons and the memory of him turned a three-fingered first baseman's ball glove into an eight-week holiday of anticipation and labor of love. I'll tell you, no mitt since has been soaped, shaped, and cared for with quite the love I gave that glove. It was important. It was a present money could not have afforded. It was provided by the memory of a father's time, concern, and love.

We all have a responsibility to provide for ourselves and for those who depend on us. "But if any provide not for his own," the apostle Paul writes, "and specially for those of his own house, he hath denied the faith, and is worse than an infidel." (1 Timothy 5:8.) Even an infidel, even a man with no faith in Christ or Christ's gospel, may love and provide for his family. How much greater, then, is the Latter-day Saint father's responsibility?

Now, I am certain that Paul did not mean to suggest that anyone should become a slave to affluence and the acquisition of material luxuries. We know too much of Paul's willing sacrifice of creature comforts to ever suspect him of greed. And it is important to note that Paul does not direct us to attend to our own appetites or needs, but to "provide" for the welfare of our house or kindred—our wife, children, and, if need be, parents.

But providing may not be as easy as it first appears. A change of attitude for us and our family toward work, stewardship of property, use of money, responsibility, and indebtedness is required if we are to fulfill the role of provider.

One of the first commandments given to Father Adam concerned work. Even in Eden, we are told, man was placed in the garden "to dress it and to keep it." (Genesis 2:15.) From the beginning, work has been a principle of growth and dignity. There is a key to be found in this; only when we are convinced of the integrity of our own work and of its necessity not only as a livelihood but also as a spiritual principle, only then will we begin to understand the full significance of providing.

I particularly dislike weed pulling. I grew up on a farm, and as a result of my long hours spent as a boy in the fields, yard work is simply not at the top of my recreational activities list. But one day, while I was working in my yard, the words "Dress this garden; take good care of it" came into my mind. Now I want to tell you that my heart began to pound—not a snare-drum titter, either, but a bass thumping—and a change came into my life. My attitude concerning the work I had so dreaded was totally new. "I'm not pulling weeds," I thought, "I'm not cleaning the yard, but, rather, I'm dressing my garden. *This* is *my* Eden. This is my stewardship. It belongs to *me*." What a difference this new thinking has made in my life. Suddenly it is not a matter of having to work, but of being allowed to work.

And yet even work, the noble responsibility given to Adam and inherited by us all, can be twisted so as to hurt more than help. "But I did it for you and the children." How often have these words been used by a delinquent father to justify his having spent more time building a career than a family. Some things money can buy—perhaps most things. But it is important for a father to remember that there are a number of less tangible realities for which money is a poor substitute. Can money teach a boy to throw a ball, a daughter of a father's love, a wife of a husband's tenderness and concern? "Thy money perish with thee," Peter said to Simon the sorcerer, "because thou hast thought that the gift of God may be purchased with money." (Acts 8:20.) There are, unhappily, fathers who make the same mistake about their families that Simon made about the priesthood—they presume to purchase with their money that which money is powerless to procure.

I'll never forget the years and years of planning our home—eight years of anxiety, a ream of graph paper, hundreds of home magazines, until finally we were able to buy the lot, construct the house, and move in. My wife and I stood in the middle of a living room still fresh with the smell of new carpet and looked at each other, as if to say, "Why is everything still the same? This was supposed to have been *it*. This was supposed to have made us happy." The prophet Jacob wrote:

> . . . *after ye have obtained a hope in Christ ye shall obtain riches, if ye seek them; and ye will seek them for the intent to do good—to clothe the naked, and to feed the hungry, and to liberate the captive, and administer relief to the sick and the afflicted.* (*Jacob 2:19.*)

Remember, while money may be used by a righteous priesthood leader to accomplish the ends suggested by Jacob, it may also be used by Satan to lead us away from the accomplishment of those goals. "No man can serve two masters. . . . Ye cannot serve God and Mammon." (Matthew 6:24.) Hence the difference between tithes and mammon: one represents a man's devotion to God, the other his service to Satan. When a man deserts his responsibility to provide for all of his family's needs for no better reason than to financially indulge his appetite, there can be no question as to whom he serves.

This has largely to do with the use of money, I suspect. Once we learn what Jacob was trying to teach us, that the only Godly use of money is to bless people's lives, then we run little risk of money's becoming mammon to our soul. Tithing may have been established by the Lord as much for this purpose as for any. Only when we are willing to sacrifice our money to God are we certain which is the more important in our lives. And it follows that if we would truly serve God with our fortunes, however large or small, then we will likewise serve our fellows, our brothers who are less blessed than we are. This is the meaning of charity as Paul preached it (see 1 Corinthians 13), and it has nothing to do with the money we give. Rather, it has to do with that which is most important in our lives—God and his children or Satan and his.

If I am charitable, if I have the "pure love of Christ" as the defining quality of my soul, there will never be a question as to whether money or people are the more important to me. If I am financially blessed, I will be led to bless my family and, as I am able, whoever may stand in need of my assistance. If, as is the case with most of us, I don't have so much money that its abundance is likely to canker my soul, then I will understand that money is like the color of one's hair—that it is not necessarily a defining characteristic—and I will no more hate my brother for his wealth than he will despise me for my poverty. We are not united by the color of our hair nor the size of our wallets, but by our love for one another and for God. This is what a father and mother must agree on and teach their children. Having done so, money—its presence or absence—can never threaten them again.

There is, of course, a considerable difference between providing for needs and indulging appetites, and we must be certain to recognize the need that our family has for individual responsibilities.

If we are to provide for our family, we must be financially able to do so. Privation and debt are poor companions to family harmony, and we must assume the responsibility of providing, to the best of our ability, a family income. This income must be generated from our ability to work, not from our capacity to borrow. Until we are free of debt, we are bound to money in a terrifying fashion—not bound to the *love* of money as are the greedy, but bound to *money*. Man was made to serve God, not an inanimate symbol of Satan's power; and so it is that we have been counseled, and are here counseled again, to avoid debt, to avoid that final possibility for money's power to corrupt.

If we are truly to be providers, we must work and teach our family members to work. We must understand and practice the law of stewardship and provide opportunities for them to learn the proper use of money. Through this insistence on individual responsibility, we will not only be able to avoid the influence of avarice or debt in our own life, but we will prepare our children against it as well.

Thus the father as provider has a real responsibility to feed, clothe, and shelter his family. But after the essentials, the greatest of all responsibilities is to provide time for and with our family and to provide them with what money cannot buy—their very own daddy who is a real father.

Chapter 10

FATHERS COMMITTED

When King Benjamin had finished his great address to the people of Zarahemla, the people all cried with one voice, saying:

Yea, we believe all the words which thou hast spoken unto us; and also, we know of their surety and truth, because of the Spirit of the Lord Omnipotent, which has wrought a mighty change in us, or in our hearts, that we have no more disposition to do evil, but to do good continually.

And we, ourselves, also, through the infinite goodness of God, and the manifestations of his Spirit, have great views of that which is to come; and were it expedient, we could prophesy of all things.

And it is the faith which we have had on the things which our king has spoken unto us that has brought us to this great knowledge, whereby we do rejoice with such exceeding great joy.

And we are willing to enter into a covenant with our God to do his will, and to be obedient to his commandments in all things that he shall command us, all the remainder of our days, that we may not bring upon ourselves a never-ending torment, as has been spoken by the angel, that we may not drink out of the cup of the wrath of God. (Mosiah 5:2-5.)

The people changed—they became sons and daughters of Christ. They made a covenant. As fathers, we must also make this covenant to ourselves, to our Heavenly Father, to Jesus Christ, and to our families. We must change! When we are truly converted to Christ and committed to living his principles, then our actions will reflect our commitment. Our responsibility, stewardship, and family goals will become our greatest challenge and the source of our happiness. This magnificent and glorious opportunity is ours if only we will take it. Fathers, arise!

For Wives: How to help your husbands to be true patriarchs

Shakespeare wisely wrote, "He is the half part of a blessed man left to be finished by such as she."

Ah, how valuable is the wife in our life!

The thrust of this book has been to help us as fathers to awaken to our responsibilities and our blessings as true patriarchs in the home. The thrust of this chapter is to help our wives help us become so, because the real success in such a venture seems to be almost in direct proportion to the woman by our side—our partner for eternity. The gospel of Jesus Christ teaches us that the way to celestial life is not unilateral.

How can a wife help her husband be an even better man, a wiser father, a more powerful patriarch? What does such a man need and want in a woman?

There are at least two classic examples of the Lord's counsel in this matter. One is God's instruction to Eve when he chastised her for eating the forbidden fruit and then explained to her, ". . . thy desire shall be to thy husband, and he shall rule over thee." (Moses 4:22.)

The second example is that tender and valuable direction the Lord gave to Emma, wife of the Prophet Joseph Smith. A careful reading of section 25 in the Doctrine and Covenants gives superb guidelines for a woman to follow so that both she and her husband can be blessed with all that God has in store for his righteous children. Though the counsel is directed to Emma, it applies to all wives. For example, consider the following excerpts:

> ... *thou art an elect lady, whom I have called. ...*
> *And the office of thy calling shall be for a comfort unto*
> *... thy husband, in his afflictions, with consoling words,*
> *in the spirit of meekness. ... lay aside the things of this*
> *world, and seek for the things of a better. ... Wherefore,*
> *lift up thy heart and rejoice, and cleave unto the*
> *covenants which thou hast made. Continue in the spirit*
> *of meekness, and beware of pride. Let thy soul delight in*
> *thy husband, and the glory which shall come upon him.*
> *Keep my commandments continually, and a crown of*
> *righteousness thou shalt receive.*

When the Lord sets the standards for behavior, it is for the best benefit to his children. This we must always remember!

So, if all the Eves since Adam's day would hearken to the Lord's will, then all the Adams since the Garden of Eden could be better husbands and fathers. That the Lord blesses us abundantly when we keep his commandments needs no definitive repeating here. It is good, though, to recall the vision of eternal togetherness with those we love and how joyous life is when we dwell in love, reaping the fulfillment of being of one heart and one flesh, one with God and his purposes.

It would surely seem evident that the plan of life given us by God is for us to be partners in parenting, to work side by side to see that families, not just individuals, make it back into the presence of our Heavenly Father. Leadership by a proper patriarch is vital. And this is in so many ways dependent upon his wife; not *unequal,* but as an equal, with a special and different role to play—as a mate supporting and sustaining and allowing him to be the true leader and patriarch to the family. Read Ephesians 5:22-33 for a fuller understanding of this partnership and role assignment. It is yet another clue to

73

strengthening the family. How can a woman be a true partner to her husband? She can—

1. Be a helpmeet.

When God presented Eve to Adam, he declared it was not good for man to be alone, and she was given to him as a helpmeet.

This means fasting and praying for him as well as caring and comforting, listening and loving. It means working along with him in that common cause of striving for perfection and exaltation for all the family. It means encouraging him in his priesthood assignments and giving thanks for your family's chance to serve Heavenly Father rather than complaining about it.

2. Be a trusted counselor.

What goes on between a woman and her husband is sacred. It does not honor him or their relationship to talk it over with a friend, mother, or co-worker. Marriage is God's gift in sanctity to his children. But a wife has her own rare qualities that a man needs in order to perform his priesthood and patriarch role well. And the husband doesn't have a lock on revelation for the family. All those who are faithful and obedient, inquiring of the Lord in righteousness, are heir to it. A man just has the last word when it comes to a decision!

I've learned that women have special insight and sensitivity. My wife has been a marvelous counselor to me because of these qualities and because she has always striven to put things in a way that doesn't demean either of us. She'll say things like, "I've thought a lot about this and wonder if you would consider this idea," or "Have you thought of this approach?" "Maybe we should take another look at our family's goals and pray again." A woman is close to the family and has a perspective different from a man's. Yet looking to him as the leader, the patriarch, is God's way. Counseling with him for the benefit of the family works. The principle is a true one from a Heavenly Father who loves us.

3. Be a friend.

"See! I told you so" never helped anyone—especially a husband. Two imperfect people struggling desperately to make it in marriage are bound to make a few mistakes. Self-righteousness and nagging must not be part of the game. Mutual love and respect come about through consistent effort on the part of both husband and wife. They should be best friends. Friends care. Friends are loyal and throw away the chaff while keeping the grain. That's why it is so hurtful when a wife (or husband) publicly criticizes her (his) mate. A wife is supposed to know her man best, to love him most. If she finds fault with him, what is left for others to think? A wonderful wife will find ways to kindly correct, lift, and suggest, and will do it when he is psychologically prepared to receive it.

4. Be a homemaker.

One's home can be a corner of heaven on earth regardless of its size, shape, location, and dripping taps. Orderliness and preparedness are vital, but the spirit there is what counts to a family. All the work and self-control it takes to create a heaven of what the father can provide is worth it when he and the children say, "It's good to be home." The embrace, the jam sandwich, the tuck before bed, the confidences and comforting, the patience in living above trifling things and reaching for the eternal scheme—all these and everything else a couple do in the home make a difference in their family now and forever. People tend to be like their environment. Eternity is now.

5. Be a sweetheart.

The Lord has said that a woman's desire should be to her husband first, not to her children, her friends, her house, her crafts, her church work. Sisters, when all is said and done, it is the man and the woman—husband and wife—who are left together when the children have gone, the friends have disappeared, and the house is old. Love should be deeper at the end of life than at the beginning. Heal your man with a constant outpouring of love and reverence. Love your husband most when he feels worst and may even deserve it least. Oh, how he'll make it up to you. It is the Lord's way for a couple to know eternal joy.

Yes, how valuable and important is the wife in our life, as we strive to become proper patriarchs!

And what blessings are in store for the woman who follows the Lord's counsel, whose desire is to her husband, who loves, honors, supports, and counsels with him and keeps all the commandments of God as she has covenanted to do!

Why, all that the Lord has promised in all his dealings with his children are hers. The Lord has promised, "I the Lord am bound when ye do what I say." He is bound to endow this woman and her husband with an outpouring of love and sweetness and joy and fulfillment forever, throughout all generations of time.

Wives, arise—help your husbands be a true patriarch in your home.

INDEX